ALSO BY CHAR MARGOLIS

Life: A Spiritual Intuitive's Collection of Inspirational Thoughts

*Questions from Earth, Answers from Heaven: A Psychic Intuitive's
Discussion of Life, Death, and What Awaits Us Beyond*

Discover
Your Inner
Wisdom

Using Intuition, Logic, and
Common Sense to Make Your Best Choices

Char Margolis
with Victoria St. George

A FIRESIDE BOOK
Published by Simon & Schuster
New York   London   Toronto   Sydney

Fireside
A Division of Simon & Schuster, Inc.
1230 Avenue of the Americas
New York, NY 10020

First Fireside trade paperback edition November 2008

FIRESIDE and colophon are registered trademarks of Simon & Schuster, Inc.

For information about special discounts for bulk purchases,
please contact Simon & Schuster Special Sales at 1-800-456-6798
or business@simonandschuster.com.

Designed by Jan Pisciotta

Manufactured in the United States of America

10 9 8 7 6 5 4 3 2 1

Library of Congress Cataloging-in-Publication Data
Margolis, Char.
   Discover your inner wisdom: using intuition, logic, and common sense to make your best choices / Char Margolis with Victoria St. George.
xx, 213p.; 23cm.
"A Fireside book."
1. Choice (Psychology)
I. St. George, Victoria. II. Title.
BF611.M28   2008
131—dc22   2007038347

ISBN-13: 978-0-7432-9789-9
ISBN-10:   0-7432-9789-X
ISBN-13: 978-0-7432-9790-5 (pbk)
ISBN-10:   0-7432-9790-3 (pbk)

To my parents, Herbie and Ida Margolis,
for their undying love and support

Contents

Foreword

Char Margolis is a good friend, a respected colleague, and someone whom I have admired for a long time. So when I was asked to write a blurb for the back cover of this book, I was so honored and excited that I offered to write the foreword!

When I was fifteen and embarking on my own spiritual journey—just like the one you may be on if you are reading this book—I became fascinated by psychic phenomena and spiritual philosophy. I read everything I could get my hands on that would help me to understand the world of energy in which we all live.

I met a lot of psychics on my path and realized that I was different from many of them. More important, I realized that I didn't want to be like them in any way. It seemed as if they were *acting* psychic rather than *being* psychic. They did "readings" because they had read a book about it, yet their psychic information was no greater than what you'd find in a fortune cookie.

Twenty years ago our society was not as evolved spiritually as it is today. The mainstream media wouldn't readily embrace psychic phenomena or mediumship in the same way it's now discussed. But a handful of people were educating the public about energy, intuition, and psychic abilities. And, yes, they were *talking to spirits*! One of those groundbreaking people is the author of this book, Char Margolis.

The first time I saw Char on television was on a very famous daytime talk show that featured a panel of psychics who were discussing their abilities and doing readings. I had been doing this work for maybe two years and felt confident in my own abilities. I also felt that I was a good judge of what was real and what was not.

The show took an abrupt turn when a man in the audience stood and announced that he was a "psychic buster" and was there to expose all the psychics as frauds. He whipped off his fake beard, took off his glasses, and held up his book (which he was promoting). The audience was aghast, and I winced at the energy of the whole experience. But as a professional watching this debacle, I was so thankful that I was not on that panel. I don't remember much else of what happened on the show except for the one person who turned that negative experience into a positive one—Char Margolis.

In the face of professional adversity she didn't care about herself or how she was perceived. Instead it was obvious that she cared about the process and the work she was born to do. From my recollection, by the end of the show Char took control by doing a reading that was so spot-on accurate that it counteracted the negativity of the naysayer. I found myself sitting on the edge of my chair, riveted by the way she delivered loving messages from the studio audience's relatives in spirit, all while not caring about being attacked by the cynic in the audience. I vowed that if I ever had the chance to tell her in person how much she helped me learn to stand up for myself and my psychic abilities, I would.

When *Crossing Over with John Edward* was being launched on television, the producers had a chance encounter with Char and asked what she thought about the show. She replied that she knew the show would be a tremendous success, and she was happy someone with my ability and integrity would be doing it. I knew right then that Char was not only a genuine psychic, doing this work for the right reason, but was also a genuine person.

You probably get that I like Char a lot. But I am also sharing my very personal thoughts and feelings with you because I want you to buy and read this book. Actually, I think you should buy two copies, because when you start to use the tools of intuition, apply them to your own life, and see a difference, you will want to share that experience with a loved one or friend. The information in this book is life affirming and life changing. And I believe the author is someone whom you can totally trust. Char gives us the tools to navigate and get the most out of our lives, while inspiring us in the process. That is not an easy task for one person or one book, but Char does it brilliantly!

Think about it. If you are standing in a bookstore and picked up this book, there's a reason. Your soul, higher self, spirit guides, or quite possibly one of your loved ones on the other side might have directed you to this book so you may live a more connected and fulfilled spiritual life. How cool is that? To know that you're not alone and that you have the ability to master and evolve your life?

I want to leave you with a few questions:

Why do we often say, "If there were a pill I could take to lose the weight I would just take it"? However, when we're faced with negative energies in our lives, we feel powerless.

What if this book is that spiritual remedy? What if by reading this book you develop greater understanding to help you better deal with challenges and change your life?

What if the inspiration that you receive helps you to reprogram the path you are on and assists you to evolve?

I truly don't believe in coincidence and I do believe that everything happens for a reason. We might not always be able to see that reason immediately, but in hindsight we usually allow ourselves the gift of understanding. I hope you are in a gift-giving and -receiving place in your life so you will embrace what you can create.

All the best,
John Edward

Introduction

My dream vacation to Capri, Italy, was over. I sat on the ferryboat idly watching reruns of *Jake and the Fatman* in Italian, not understanding a word. From Naples I would catch a flight to Milan and then to Munich, Germany, where I would stay overnight and then board a plane for the United States. I was anxious to get home to America and share with my family and friends my adventures in Europe, which had included an appearance on a German talk show. As a spiritual intuitive and teacher of intuition, I also had a full schedule of readings, media appearances, and seminars waiting for me at home.

When I arrived at the airport in Munich, I found that one of my bags was lost. I said to the airport attendant (who spoke perfect English), "No problem—just send the bag on to the United States, as I'll be leaving Europe tomorrow."

She shook her head. "Impossible," she said.

Maybe she didn't understand me, I thought. I don't speak German, so I made my request in English again, trying to enunciate and explain my situation to her clearly.

She interrupted me. "Didn't you hear? The World Trade Center and the Pentagon were attacked."

"What?" I said, not registering her words at first. "You mean in New York and in Washington?"

"Yes," the woman answered. "The towers were hit by two jetliners. The World Trade Center is gone. All air travel to and from the United States is canceled until further notice."

I left the terminal in shock. Because I have been working as a psychic intuitive for almost thirty years, I realize that no psychic receives warnings about every major event, but I couldn't believe such a thing could occur to my country without my tuning in to it in advance. Then I remembered a premonition I had had a year earlier about my good friends and clients, Mike and Chris Blackman. Mike had worked for a very successful New York firm and was in charge of opening their new offices in the World Trade Center. In 2000 during a psychic reading I had told Mike and Chris, "If you're thinking of leaving New York, you should do it soon. I feel strongly that there will be a terrorist attack in the near future." They had followed my advice and relocated to San Diego, California. Mike told me later that there was a very good chance that he would have been in the World Trade Center that day if he still worked in New York. "I'm convinced that your suggestion saved my life," he said.

Looking at the horrific photos of the collapsing towers in a German newspaper on September 12, I thought, *Why didn't I predict this? Why didn't I sense this was going to happen while I was in Italy?* Then suddenly I remembered. In 1999 I had hosted a television special in the United States and I was asked if I had any predictions for the new millennium. "The one thing I always worry about is chemical warfare, biological warfare, and terrorism in our country," I said. "I also sense that the airports will be involved in this problem; the governments should look to securing our airports better." Of course, in 1999 no one in the United States was thinking seriously about terrorism, much less terrorism by airplane. But in 2001 things would be very different. It wasn't until two weeks after September 11 that I was finally able to fly back to my country, which would never be the same.

Where do such intuitive messages come from? And why do I get them? As to "why me?" I have no idea. From an early age I was able to pick up on other people's energy. When I was four years old I came back from the grocery store and announced, "Mommy, the lady cheated us!" It turned out the cashier had shortchanged my father. I saw my first spirit at age eight, and by my teenage years I was advising my friends about their relationships.

In my early twenties, I began to study intuition and how to develop my psychic abilities. I decided that I wasn't going to be like psychics who gave very general information; I was going to be *specific*. I developed a method of tuning in to the initials and names of those on the other side. At the time, this approach was very unusual; in fact, author and radio personality Sally Jessy Raphael called me the "alphabet soup psychic" because nobody else was doing what I did.

For more than thirty years I have been giving readings to people all over the world and teaching others to access their own sixth sense. I wrote my first book, *Questions from Earth, Answers from Heaven,* to share with everyone my method for developing and accessing our innate, God-given gift of intuition. As a spiritual intuitive, I do my best to help people prevent problems and attain goals in their lives. I feel and read the energy that comes from people, the planet, and the universe. I also communicate with the spirit world. I'm known for my ability to reach across the barrier that separates this world from the next and put people in touch with loved ones who have crossed over. These spirits give me names and information that I could never get otherwise, proving to those who are still on earth that love never dies and love serves as the bridge between us and the world beyond. I am continually humbled by and grateful for the privilege of helping others connect with the people they love most.

I love doing readings for people and bringing them advice and consolation, but I've come to believe that my true mission on earth is to *awaken people to their own inborn, intuitive power*. You see, most of us are ignoring one of the senses that God gave us: our sixth sense, or intuition. Like our other senses, intuition is essential to our making our way successfully in the world. If you've ever felt afraid for no reason when walking down a deserted street, or found yourself thinking of someone you haven't heard from for a long time only to get an e-mail or an unexpected phone call from that person, or followed a hunch to play a particular number in a game of chance and had it win, or suddenly worried about your child and later discovered he hurt himself at school that day, then you have experienced the power of your intuition.

We've been taught to use our common sense to evaluate the choices we're offered, and to apply logic to help us weigh the pros and cons. But seldom do we tap into the power that I believe is equally important in helping us make the wisest choice in any moment—intuition.

My students and clients say that they make better choices when they use their intuition. Intuition can take you places logic and common sense never will. And when you combine logic, common sense, *and* intuition, you'll make even wiser choices.

I believe that we discount our intuition at our peril. How many of us have ignored our inner warnings about a relationship, a job, an individual, or a situation, only to find to our sorrow that our intuition was right on? How many people who died in the World Trade Center that September day had a feeling not to go into work but decided to disregard such "foolishness"? On the other hand, there were people at the World Trade Center who were told to go back into the second building "for their own safety," but they refused because they felt it was too dangerous. They went against the authorities who were running the scene and they survived while thousands died. Was this just common sense? Maybe. But as my mother used to say, common sense isn't all that common. More important, these people listened to their instincts and lived to talk about it.

Intuition works in other ways, too. When we set our minds and hearts on something we want to manifest, we attune ourselves to its presence and begin to subconsciously—"intuitively"—welcome it into our reality. Intuition tunes us in to the currents of the universal energy, helping us to tap into a power greater than ourselves to create what we want and prevent potential problems. Intuition is a powerful tool for manifesting the good and the bad, for avoiding danger and protecting ourselves. By discovering your inner wisdom, your inner intuition, you will learn how to use this powerful force to attract what you desire, repel what you do not, and have the wisdom to know the difference.

What Is Intuition?

As one scientist defined it, intuition is "the process of reaching accurate conclusions based on inadequate information." Intuition can transcend time and space. It's capable of telling you which is the right or wrong decision at the split second you have to make it. It's the power that says, "Go talk to that person," who later turns out to have just the right information for your success, or becomes a good friend or a trusted colleague. Intuition is like a golden pillar that lies at the core of our being. It holds everything together and supports us in making the best decisions for our lives. Like many golden treasures, it's hidden; it must be discovered and actively used for it to make a difference in our everyday lives.

There's a difference between intuition at random and intuition on demand. Intuition at random is when the universe gives you the little nudging thoughts in the course of your everyday life that lead you in a certain direction. Maybe you get home and put the groceries on the kitchen table and something tells you to go look for your insurance folder. You do so and find out your insurance payment is due the next day and somehow you mislaid this month's bill. Random intuition occurs when, for whatever reason, we dip into that universal energy and receive a message pointing us in the right direction or warning us of danger.

When the universe is giving you a message, your responsibility is to be aware of it, listen to what it says, and then follow through. But it's also possible to ask questions and get answers, accessing that universal energy through your intuition. That's a big part of the intuition you can use to manifest what you want in your life.

Recently the book and the movie *The Secret* have been very popular because they teach people to tap into the energy of the universe to help them attain their desires. But I also believe that we need to be sensitive to the bigger picture of how our desires fit into the universe's wishes for us. If you've ever worked incredibly hard at manifesting something with no results, you may be like a cosmic "salmon" trying to swim upstream against the current of universal energy. Sometimes no matter how much we work to manifest our desires, we don't get the Cadillac or the perfect house or the perfect relationship. While we have free choice and not everything is predestined, there are certain events in store for us that we either will experience or, perhaps, use our intuition to avoid. Intuition can help us ask for what we want, check to see if our desires are attuned with universal energy, and then point our efforts in the right direction to take advantage of the powerful current.

However, if you want to be intuitive, you have to suspend your disbelief. That is, you must believe it is possible to hear the whispers of your inner voice. Intuition is like a phone call with you on one end of the phone and the universe on the other. The universe can keep calling and calling and calling, but you have to answer the phone! When you take the first step of believing in your own inner wisdom, you will find a universe eager to open its vast storehouse of knowledge to you.

The first four chapters describe how to develop your "intuitive asking" skills, so you can tap into this powerful source of information to make your life better. In chapters 5 through 10, I show you how to use your intuition to read the universal energy signals in several important areas of your life: relationships, sex, health, work, finances, and children. Some of what you read in these pages will challenge the way you think, because it's a challenge to think outside the box. But if I can prove to you that the "box" is a lot bigger than you thought, the opportunities available to you become a lot larger, too.

Intuition won't take away all your problems; there are some things we have to face for our own growth. Life is a school and we're all here to learn important lessons before we can "graduate" to a higher level. But once you learn to use it, intuition can and will show you what the universe has in store for you and help you make the best decisions in the moment. The real "secret" lies within your ability to listen to your intuition to make good choices about what you do and don't wish to attract.

Your inner wisdom is an immense power—it gives you access to all the power and goodness and love of the entire universe. It also makes you aware of the negative energies (yes, they exist) that wish to trick you. The key to using your intuition is to be aware of its power, respect it, and learn to use it with good intentions for yourself and others. With some preparation, intention, and above all, a desire to align with the goodness, love, and wisdom of the universe, your inner wisdom can guide you and give you the abundant, loving, and joyous life you desire.

1

The Magic Within and Around You

I have the best job on earth—I help people speak with their loved ones on the other side, and I also teach people to use their gift of intuition. Daily I have the opportunity to hear the joy and relief when a person's departed loved one speaks through me, communicating the most powerful message of all: love never dies. And almost as often I have the opportunity to watch as people tap into their own inner wisdom—the ultimate guide that can show us how to experience more love, happiness, health, and success.

Whenever I give readings, people ask me where I get my information. "How can you walk down the street, pick out perfect strangers, and tell them exactly what's going on in their lives?" they say. "How can you not only tell them about their deceased relatives but also give them solid, concrete advice about their love lives or finances or health? How can you be so accurate?" The answer is simple: I can see and feel the different kinds of energy around a person. We each have our own energy "thumbprint" that identifies us as who we are in this lifetime. How we live our lives, the choices we make, and how we act and react shape that energy thumbprint. When you can read an energy thumbprint like I can, it's pretty easy to know what's going on with people. I know whether they're happy in love or successful in their careers. I can feel the energy of spirits and angels from the other side who are with them. I can sense when danger is coming, when someone has unseen health challenges, and whether or not someone is good at attracting and keeping money. This ability to sense unseen energy is what intuition is all about. It works by putting us in touch with the life force that unites us all.

Intuition works by tapping into the energy of the universe. Everything—every being, plant, stone, body of water, star, even the air we breathe—has a power, an energy, contained within it. We are all connected at the deepest level because we are all part of the same stuff. This energetic life force can be you, me, the floor, the air, your unborn child, and your long-dead grandmother—it's all part of the same energy. This unifying energy is being investigated by experiments in quantum physics, which is some of the most complicated and intriguing science being done today. I don't even pretend to understand what these scientists are up to, but certain experiments have shown that every atom and molecule in the universe is connected. And human beings are as much a part of this energy as everything else.

The human body and psyche can sense the powerful forces of energy that compose the universe because the same energy flows through us; it is part of our connection to the world and beyond. Traditional Chinese medicine tells us this energy, or *qi,* runs through our bodies via channels called "meridians." When we reach puberty we feel this energy in terms of sexual attraction. We pick up on the energy of a particular place and decide if this is somewhere we wish to settle. Tuning in to the energy around us is hardwired into the nervous system of every animal, including us. Why do you think pets can seem to read our emotions, especially when we're upset or depressed? Why are animals the first to warn us when there's an earthquake or other natural disaster? I was fascinated to learn that when the tsunami devastated the coastlines of many countries along the Indian Ocean in December 2004, rescuers went into a wild animal park in Sri Lanka expecting to find a high death toll among the animals. Instead, almost no animals were killed by the tsunami. The elephants, tigers, monkeys, and many other species had sensed the tsunami long enough before it struck to make it to higher ground. How did the animals escape while so many human beings died? Had the animals felt the vibrations of an earthquake over a thousand miles distant? Had the energy of the water rushing toward the land thrummed through the seabed to the island of Sri Lanka? We will never know—but the animals did.

As human beings with thinking brains, most of us discount our own innate "animal" ability to sense the energy in ourselves, in others, and in our environment. But more and more of us are coming to believe in and use this natural sixth sense. We are recognizing the value of intuition and how it puts us in touch with forces far beyond what we can perceive with our conscious minds.

Intuition Equals Reading Energy

Intuition lets us tune in to the little "energy signals" we get from the universe. For instance, you're thinking of a deceased loved one and the lights flicker. Or you have a psychic or intuitive "hit" that you should apply for another job even though you like where you are, and the next week your boss leaves and his replacement is a real jerk. Or you feel there's a change coming, and a woman knocks on your door and says, "Do you want to sell your house?" There's no For Sale sign and you haven't listed your house with anyone, but the woman offers you such a good deal that you take it immediately. Or maybe a friend invites you to a party. Normally you hate parties where you don't know anyone, but for some reason this time you feel it's important to go. You walk into the party and within five minutes you meet the person you end up marrying.

We've all seen individuals who seem to be able to connect with different aspects of the universal life force. I believe that these "lucky" individuals are better at reading and connecting with the life force that exists in each of us and in everything in the universe. But *all* human beings have been given a tremendous gift by our Creator: we can use our intuition to make our lives better. With intention and practice, we can learn to understand and tap into the different kinds of energy in our lives. For instance:

- You've had a run of bad relationships—you have a habit of attracting people with the same dysfunctional energy. What if your intuition could help you find the man or woman of your dreams?

- You've been laid off from work or you're stuck in a job with no possibility of advancement. What if you could intuitively sense the job that will be perfect for you, or use your inner wisdom to navigate difficult situations and deal with difficult people at your current workplace?

* Your retirement account has been slashed in half by a bad turn in the stock market. What if you could choose winning investments and investment advisors by combining intuition, common sense, and a little research?

* You've had a pain in your side for a few days but your spouse tells you not to worry about it. What if you could use your intuitive sense of your body to know whether to call the doctor, go to the emergency room, or just go to bed?

* With all the events of the past few years, you're worried about your children's safety as well as your own. What if you could teach your children how to sense the energy in any situation or any other person, to accurately assess the presence of danger, and to get themselves out of risky situations before trouble arrives?

These are just a few of the ways that you can learn to use your inner wisdom to sense and direct the universal life force to change your life for the better. With practice, you can learn to combine the powers of your conscious and instinctual minds to create an energy "signal" that will draw to you the people and events you want in your life. You can then redirect the currents of the life force simply through your will and intention. You will become an active collaborator with universal energy in creating the life you desire.

A wonderful Japanese man, Masaru Emoto, is known for photographing ice crystals composed of water that comes from many different sources all over the planet. He exposes the water to different words—like *love and gratitude* or *I hate you,* for example—then photographs the crystals formed by that water. Water exposed to the words *love and gratitude* forms beautiful, symmetrical crystals, while the water exposed to the words *I hate you* produces deformed blobs.

What I found most interesting, however, was an experiment done by a Japanese family that knows of Emoto's work. They took three jars of rice and put them out in the house. Every day the family would say "Thank you" to one jar of rice and "You fool" to another. The third jar of rice they ignored altogether. After a month, the "Thank you" rice had started to ferment, producing a smell like malt. The "You fool" rice had rotted and turned black. And the rice that was ignored rotted even faster than the "You fool" rice!

I think our intuition is like those jars of rice. If we say we don't believe in it or ignore its warnings, it will eventually stop trying to signal us and we can find ourselves in very serious trouble. Like the rice, our intuition will prosper when we put our intention and attention on it.

Coincidences Are Signals from the Universe

When it comes to making choices in our lives, it's important to know what to look for. Many times the universe signals us through what some people call "coincidences." You decide to put your three-bedroom house on the market and before you can tell anyone or even contact a Realtor, a friend calls and says, "My sister's having a baby and they need a bigger place. Do you know of any three-bedroom houses in your area?" You're wondering how your child's doing in school and that afternoon his teacher sends home a note about Johnny's progress in math. You drive down the same road every day on your way to work, and one day you notice a sign saying Pass with Care. You don't remember ever seeing that sign before and you think nothing of it—until a few minutes later you get ready to change lanes to pass a car in front of you when you hear a horn blaring from that lane, and you just barely avoid being sideswiped by a speeding SUV. Is it a coincidence or is it synchronicity? Is it just a joke the universe is playing on you? Maybe—but far more likely such occurrences are instances of the universe stepping in to warn us, take care of us, and show us whether or not we are in tune.

Life is like a treasure hunt, and the universe is always supplying us with clues on how to find our treasures. Some clues come in the form of coincidences. Years ago I had been involved with a man, but I hadn't seen or talked to him in six months. One day I had a feeling to travel down a certain road in Michigan, where I had lived at the time. Guess who was coming my way in the other lane? He spotted me, jumped out of his car, and flagged me down. Our meeting rekindled the relationship, and I ended up marrying him. I hadn't developed my intuitive gift at that point in my life, but I feel that the coincidence of running into him was due to my sensing the currents in the energy of the universe. As I have learned through the years, if we're smart we pay attention to those coincidences so we can attune our lives to what the universe wants of and for us.

I've heard too many stories from people about the meaningful coincidences in their lives, and experienced too many coincidental messages in mine, to discount the fact that the universe is always trying to show us what's coming. It's just a matter of our noticing and interpreting what the universe has to say. A chance event can lead us onto a path of divine intervention. Coincidence also may teach us a lesson to "be aware" of something even though it looks like it is "meant to be." I heard a story once of a woman who was getting ready to move to California to be with her boyfriend of about a year. She was having lunch with a few girlfriends when one of them said, "A client of mine mentioned a man with the same name as your boyfriend—only this guy has a wife in Miami, Florida! Strange, huh?" Very strange, since the woman's boyfriend had lived in Miami for several years but never mentioned being married before. The woman did some research and found that her boyfriend did indeed have a wife and several children in Florida, as well as a failed business and hundreds of thousands of dollars in debts. She confronted her boyfriend, he admitted everything, and she called off the move.

Coincidences can confirm that we're going in the right direction, as in the example of wanting to put your house on the market and getting a call from a friend whose sister wants to buy one. They also can tell us our plans are not in sync with the universe, and we need to pay attention to those promptings, too. Suppose you decided you wanted to take a vacation to England with a friend. You were all ready to book the flight, but you opened the newspaper and the first thing you noticed was a headline in the travel section that read ENGLAND—NO! IRELAND—YES! Later your friend calls and says, "I've just gotten an invitation to speak at a conference in Ireland. Would you consider coming over and making that our vacation?" It should be pretty clear to you that Ireland, not England, is your "universally" approved destination!

You may not recognize a coincidence until something happens more than once. When I was preparing for a TV show in the United States, one of the producers suggested we do a piece on using magnets for healing. That same day, I ran into two people at different times, both of whom told me (without my asking or bringing up the subject) that they were wearing magnets in their shoes. When you recognize a coincidence, sometimes you'll get a feeling of "Wow!" or awe or goose bumps. Or it may take you awhile to recognize a coincidence by making the connection between the signal and what the universe is trying to tell you.

There's a story about a man who owned a house by a river. There had been a lot of rain and the river was rising quickly. The sheriff came by and told the man he needed to evacuate, but he said, "The Lord will save me." The river kept rising until the water was up to the house's back door. A rescue boat came by and the crew called to the man, "Come with us!" But the man shook his head and said, "The Lord will save me." The water kept rising until the house was almost completely submerged. The man was sitting on the roof of his house when a helicopter flew over and tossed down a rope. "Grab on and we'll pull you up!" the crew said, but the man refused: "The Lord will save me," he said. The water kept right on rising, and the man was swept away and drowned. When he arrived in heaven, he went before the Lord and complained, "I believed you would save me, and you didn't!" The Lord replied, "I sent a sheriff, a boat, and a helicopter. What more did you need?"

We have to be careful in interpreting coincidences as signs from the universe rather than the result of other energies. For example, suppose you're in love with someone who is forbidden fruit—he's in another relationship or just plain bad for you—and you happen to run into him on the street. You could think "That's the universe saying we're meant to be together!" But it could be that your desire, not your intuition, drew that person to you even if he's no good for you. Or it could even be a trickster energy trying to lead you down the wrong path. Or it could be that this relationship is your destiny because you have to learn a very painful lesson from it. You have to use both your common sense and instinct to perceive and to understand the signals from the universe. Sometimes you may be wrong in your interpretation, but you also may be right. It's a question of doing your best to follow what you feel the universe is telling you and then seeing how things play out. With practice you'll learn to discover the meanings that coincidence offers you. And I've found that the more you try to tune in to these messages from the universe, the more frequently they'll appear in your life, and the more accurate your interpretations will be.

Connecting at the Highest Level

A big part of what I do when I read for people is pick up on the energies of spirits, guardian angels, and departed loved ones. It's part of my mission to bring closure to those who grieve, and to give them hope by showing them that love never dies and their parents, spouses, and children still exist on another level. But you can be intuitive without being spiritual or believing in spirit communication. The main purposes for developing intuition are: (1) to put us in touch with the universal consciousness that is everywhere and that is composed of goodness, love, and wisdom; and (2) to help us make better choices here on earth by tapping into a level of awareness and information (i.e., energy) that is beyond what our five senses, logic, and common sense have to offer.

I began learning this work by connecting with the spirit world. However, I learned very early to go to the highest level of universal consciousness and oneness for guidance. Intuition is like a receiver that can be tuned to different frequencies. At one level it can link us to guides and spirits of those who have passed over. Contacting spirits on the other side is important because it takes away our fear of death. But speaking with spirits is only part of using our intuition. Intuition is also our means of connecting to something much greater than any individual soul or spirit. It is our way of connecting with the universal energy source, the fount of all wisdom, guidance, and abundance.

To gain the best guidance, you want to go to a more powerful level, the highest plane of goodness, love, and wisdom. We are all connected to this higher wisdom because we are made of its energy. This is not religion; I'm not going to get into the debate over whether God exists or what form God takes. I was always taught that God is love and love is God. But I do know that when I use my intuition or teach others to do so, I always ask that my information come from the highest energy level of goodness, love, and wisdom. That's where I believe we are all united and part of the same great energy. Universal consciousness lies inside each one of us, and we can ask it for guidance using our intuition.

When we consider the law of attraction, a well-known divine principle, we can understand that all things come through the energy of thought, which is the energy of intuition. In fact, there is nothing in this world that did not begin with a thought.

Life is much easier when you use your intuition to connect to the level of energy, of spirit, of creation. When we step out of our confinement in the world of everyday reality and tap into the universal life force of which we are a part, and when we learn to use our intuition and will to direct our thoughts and actions, then we become partners in our destiny at the deepest level.

If you are studying intuition for the first time, you may not find this journey easy. The road less taken is always an uphill climb. But after thirty years, I can guarantee you that the climb is definitely worth it. With practice and by combining intuition with intention, you can use your intuition to make your life, and the lives of those around you, far more fulfilling. Your life can be like that of scientist Jonas Salk, who wrote "It is always with excitement that I wake up in the morning wondering what my intuition will toss up to me, like gifts from the sea. I work with it and rely on it. It's my partner." With intuition as your partner, you can harness the highest power of the universe to help you in every step of your journey through life.

2

Tapping the Power of
Your Intuition

*Whether revealing the hard truth about toxic relationships, your
exhaustion level, or a thankless job, intuition is always trying
to communicate, though you may not hear. It resides in a quiet
place obscured by the chatter of everyday thoughts.*

—Judith Orloff, M.D., intuitive

Everyone's experience of intuition is different. One of the
easiest ways to begin to recognize your own sixth sense is
by tuning in to someone else's unique energy signature—his or
her "thumbprint." Have you ever been in a room with your back
toward the door and, without hearing a voice, you knew who
walked into the room? It could be your father, mother, lover,
son, daughter, friend, cat, or dog, but you knew exactly who it
was because you felt their energy. Any kind of strong emotional
connection can enhance our ability to sense someone's energy
thumbprint. Imagine that you're a parent of three children who
are close to one another in age. One of your children comes

up behind you and puts her hands over your eyes. Can you tell which child it is? Most parents say that they know instantly who's playing the game, because each of their children "feel" different. Their different personalities produce different energies.

We can also sense not just the energy but also the emotions of another person. Have you ever been in a great mood and then stood next to someone whose vibes were weird? Perhaps you were at a party, in the office, or on a bus, subway, or train. Maybe the person you were standing next to was sad or miserable. Maybe he was mad at someone. But without either of you saying a word, you could read his emotional state. We also can see this in action with the people closest to us. Mothers, don't you usually know what your babies and young children are feeling, even when they can't tell you directly? And how many times have you walked into the house from work and known something was up with your partner, even before a word was spoken between you?

I've been teaching people to use their intuition for a long time, and I can tell pretty quickly whether or not someone is aware of her innate sixth sense. But anyone can become more sensitive to intuitive promptings. For example, I once did a workshop for a group of account managers at Microsoft. This was not a group you would consider as being very in tune with their intuitive side! Yet by the end of the workshop, one of the gentlemen was picking up on information about my family, and he was very accurate in his statements about them. (He also mentioned the last name of someone who he said would be interviewing me in the near future, and said that it would be a tough interview. He was right!)

Most intuitive experiences aren't designed to help you talk with spirits or your departed loved ones (although you may become more sensitive to their energies). Most intuitions are not "mind reading" either. I do believe that there are individuals who can read minds, picking up thoughts and impressions from others. About twenty years ago, a gentleman called "The Amazing Kreskin" did mind-reading shows in the United States, and during each show the producers would hide his paycheck and he'd have to read their minds to find it! But the intuition I teach people to access is about tuning in at a much higher level, receiving information from sources that go far beyond individual consciousness. Almost every time I read for someone, I'll bring up a name and the person will say, "I haven't thought of him or her for years!" Or I'll say something like, "Fernando is here for you," and my client won't know who that is, only to discover that Fernando is the real name of the great-uncle whom they only knew as Buster, or perhaps he is a brother who died before the client was born. That kind of information isn't coming from the person sitting in front of me; it's being given to me from the level of spirit, and ultimately from universal consciousness.

Intuition also can come in the form of feelings. You may get into a business deal and get a bad feeling about one of the partners. Maybe at the same time the thought pops into your head "Be careful of David, he's a weak link." Or maybe you're at home and from out of nowhere you feel uneasy about your spouse and you think, *Hmmm, I wonder where Mary is right now.* We've all had the experience of feeling we shouldn't trust someone even if we've just met him, or we sense the situation we're in is not going to turn out well. Conversely, there are times when we feel everything is going our way and we can trust the people we're with.

To become aware of the untapped power of your own intuition, start by remembering when it was active. Take a moment and recall at least one time you believe your intuition was speaking to you. Maybe you ran into a good friend and without saying a word, you knew what your friend was feeling. Maybe you felt there was going to be a hitch in a project at work even though all the signs were good, and lo and behold, it tanked. Maybe you were thinking of an old boyfriend or girlfriend and one minute later "your" song came on the radio. Maybe you were speeding along the highway and you had the feeling you'd better slow down and watch out, and as a result you were driving the speed limit when you passed the police car waiting around the next curve in the road. (I can't tell you how many times that little warning feeling has helped me avoid a speeding ticket!) There are so many ways the universe is using our intuition to speak to us, and acknowledging the times we've heard its messages will help us notice the next message that comes along. Later in this book you'll learn a step-by-step process you can use to access your intuition to answer questions and provide guidance for your life.

The Power of Thoughts

Our thoughts can either help or hinder the development of our intuition. Thoughts are a powerful force in the universe. Thoughts are things. They create our reality. They are energy waves used to communicate with the living and with those in the spirit world. They're also the gatekeepers to our minds: they can bar the door and keep us from ever using the enormous power of our sixth sense, or they can open the gates so we can put our intuition to work.

Have you ever read about people who are hypnotized and told that when they wake up, they will not be able to see? When they're taken out of trance, you can flash bright lights to make their eyes react, but they'll still declare without hesitation that they're completely blind. Their subconscious minds are blocking their ability to see. It's the same with our intuition: we all have it, but we can block our perception of what it has to tell us simply by thinking we aren't intuitive. With our intuition, however, it's the subconscious mind that's active and the conscious mind that creates the block. Caroline Myss is a woman I admire greatly—she's a medical intuitive and has written several books about intuition, archetypes, and sacred psychology. She says, "Receiving intuitive information or guidance is effortless. What is difficult is removing your fears about what your intuition is telling you." Our thoughts and fears can hold us back from using our sixth sense.

If you think "Intuition is a lot of garbage; it's just trying to make meanings from coincidence and hindsight," you're allowing your thoughts to hypnotize you, and you'll never even notice the occasions when your inner wisdom is trying to give you a sign. However, if you hold yourself open to the possibility that intuition exists and you possess the same sixth sense as every other human being on the planet, then these thoughts will allow your intuition to do what it was meant to: guide you, give you warnings, and connect you to the vast wisdom of the universe. So start your journey by looking at yourself in the mirror and saying ten times, "Like every other person in the world, I am intuitive!" Own it and know it, even if you have no proof. It might take a little effort to make you aware of what you're already seeing but don't yet recognize as your intuitive sense.

One of the most important aspects of developing your intuition is to become aware of your thoughts. When I read for people (and I've heard my great friend, psychic John Edward, say the same is true for him), I feel their energy first, and then I tune in and start getting messages in the form of thoughts that I know are not mine. These messages just pop into my head; they not only are information I have no way of knowing, but they also *feel* different. For you to learn the difference between everyday thoughts and intuitive messages, you need to spend quiet time becoming aware of your thoughts. Even five minutes a day focusing on your thoughts is enough to increase your sensitivity to your intuition.

Becoming aware of your thoughts is essential not only to develop your intuition but also to maintain your psychological and emotional health. Negative thoughts attract negative thoughts and positive thoughts attract positive thoughts. It's all too easy for us to get into bad habits when it comes to our thoughts, especially when they're about ourselves and our abilities. Doubting thoughts, negative thoughts, self-critical thoughts will all block us from using our intuition to its fullest potential. Thoughts that are positive, uplifting, focused on what's possible rather than what might go wrong will tend to keep our channels open and clear the way for intuitive thoughts to come in. Norman Vincent Peale was right when he wrote about the power of positive thinking, because positive thoughts keep us healthier and more balanced. I'm not saying be a Pollyanna and act like everything's great even when things go wrong; we all have to be realistic. However, realistic is not the same thing as pessimistic. Use the power of your thoughts to keep yourself focused on the best outcome no matter what the situation.

The Difference Between Intuition,
Experience, Desire, and Wishful Thinking

Some psychologists believe that intuition is nothing but an experienced-based shortcut provided by our brains to help us make quick decisions. However, I believe intuition connects us to a much larger pool of wisdom—the wisdom of the entire universe. Have you ever been on a computer and wanted to find a piece of information? What's the easiest and fastest way to get what you want to know? You use a search engine: you pull up a website like Google and type in a few words. Within seconds Google searches through hundreds of millions of bits of information and then displays for you a selection of sites that comes closest to matching your request.

That's the way intuition works. It's the search engine that ties us into the 99.99 percent of the universe that we don't know about, won't ever know about consciously, and could study for the next thousand years and still wouldn't know or understand. We send out an unspoken request to the universe—"Should I take the job out of state?" "Is this the best deal?" "Which road home will have the least traffic?"—and our intuition searches through all the vast knowledge available and comes back to us with an answer.

In *The Secret,* we hear over and over that our job is simply to choose what we want and then pay attention as the universe delivers our desires. When we ask something as simple as "Which road home will have the least traffic?" what we are really asking for is a smooth, convenient, safe, and easy ride home. Our intuition is the way we tune in to what the universe offers. It can guide us in manifesting the optimal route when we pause to ask and then receive the intuitive answer that always follows.

Ralph Waldo Emerson said, "We live in the lap of an immense intelligence and we are receptors." Unfortunately, we don't have a computer screen to display our intuitive "search results"; the screen is much more subtle. Most of the time, intuition is a thought here, a feeling there, the song on the radio or goose bumps—small signals that come from outside our own conscious knowledge. Part of tapping into your own intuitive power is learning what's intuition and what's not. It can be easy to confuse intuition with our own desires; to think, *Hey, my intuition is telling me this guy is perfect for me,* when in truth you're attracted to him because he looks like the ex-boyfriend that left you for another woman. Wishful thinking can also be mistaken for intuition, where you think, *I'll bet I can make a million dollars on this deal!* and you plunge ahead without using your good, old-fashioned common sense to check things out.

Rather than being the result of intuition, our desires and wishful thinking actually can stop us from being clear receptors for the information the universe is sending us. It's like walking down the street with ear buds in and our favorite playlist running on the iPod. Our ears are filled with music and we're rocking out, but because we're "plugged in" we can't hear the birds, the wind in the trees, or the soft voice of a companion. In the same way, if we stay plugged in to our wishes and desires, we cannot hear the subtle thoughts and signals that are the voices of our sixth sense.

One of the most difficult times to get the messages from your intuition is when you need an answer to a deep-seated question that's close to your heart. It's ironic that often when we really want our intuition to work, it can be short-circuited by our own emotional attachment to getting an answer! It's like trying to give advice to someone when you're upset or you have a lot on the line—your emotions are going to get in the way of your objectivity and ability to see things clearly. You have to learn to separate yourself from the question or the situation and ask from a detached perspective. In later chapters you'll learn more about ways to pose questions to your intuition and get clear responses.

So how can you distinguish between intuition and your own thoughts, emotions, desires, and wishful thinking? When you get an intuitive feeling, it's a feeling of knowing and being at one with the universe. You're balanced and peaceful. There's a sense of it being right and you're not fooling yourself. Usually if it's a desire or wishful thinking, it'll feel different from your intuition. Intuition is almost like you're remembering the future: there's a certainty about it. It's not just a product of what your mind logically tells you might occur.

I believe in using both logic and common sense when it comes to the choices in our lives. But intuition is just as valuable as both, because it's coming from another level. Later I'll describe a method for using logic, common sense, and intuition as your guides to making wise decisions.

I'll say quite honestly, that when you first start practicing with your intuition, you'll probably make a lot of mistakes. You'll confuse genuine intuitive promptings with desires, wishful thinking, or faulty logic. Then something will happen—the job you just knew you had doesn't pan out, or the guy who you think is sending you signals in the bar gets up and walks away without talking to you—and it'll be clear that your "intuition" wasn't accurate. Congratulations! You now have the chance to learn something important. Take a few minutes to examine the feeling you had that you called intuition and see what was really going on. What caused the feeling? What was the cue you perhaps misread? Did your desire get in the way of what the universe was really telling you? Were there perhaps other signals that you missed because you were blinded by your emotions and/or wishes? Or perhaps you've had a premonition of the future, and your intuition will come true a few hours, days, or weeks from now.

Do the same kind of review with any accurate hunch or intuition. How did this intuition come to you? Was it a thought? An emotion? A sensation in your gut? A coincidence that you couldn't explain? Just as everyone's energy thumbprint is unique, everyone's intuitive style is individual and unique as well. I pick up on initials of people's names and hear thoughts that pop into my head. Other people may see something on a desk or a sign by a road, or a commercial on TV that they know is the answer to their question. I read once that one of the top art historians of the twentieth century could tell a fake because he got dizzy as soon as he saw it, before his conscious mind could do any analysis of the artwork. With practice, you, too, can discover your own intuitive style, whether thoughts come to you, or you have a feeling in your gut, or you see messages in everyday objects. As you examine your real intuitions, you'll learn what to trust and what not to trust. Then you can say to yourself either "I know I'm putting my own thoughts and words into this—this is just my desire, because I know deep inside this isn't what's right for me" or, "This isn't coming from my wishes or desires; this is really what the universe wants me to do."

Protecting Yourself from Negative
or "Trickster" Energies

When you use your intuition, you are opening yourself up to energies that can be positive, neutral, or even negative. Last year I met a psychic at the house of a girlfriend of mine. The psychic was very accurate in her reading, but she admitted that she allows trickster energies to come in when she does readings. She believes everything the spirits tell her, instead of checking what she receives by going to the highest level of consciousness. So I told my girlfriend, "She's a sweet girl and a great psychic, but you've got to be careful around her. Because if she's allowing trickster energies into her own life, the messages she gives you may not be true."

The energies you pick up could be coming from other people, from spirits, or just from the part of the world you're in. Different locations have different energies. For example, when visiting Assisi, Italy, where St. Francis lived, you can feel his gentle love permeating the cathedral where he is buried. On the other hand, entering the gates of Dachau or Auschwitz concentration camps produces an entirely different sensation—suffering, dread, death, and evil. We've all felt love from another person, and most of us also have felt negative energy like jealousy, anger, or hate from others. Even children know about the power of other people's energies. I once read for a couple whose preteen son had committed suicide. I picked up that the boy had been harassed at his school by the other children, and he was so sensitive, he hadn't been able to handle the negative energy directed toward him.

When developing your intuition, you're deliberately tuning in to energy from outside of yourself. This can bring you great benefit but also can create some risk. It's like taking out your cell phone and dialing a number. While you're talking it's just possible that signals from other calls might interfere with your conversation. Even worse, there are people out there with devices that can allow them to eavesdrop on you, jam your call, or even steal your cell phone number or download your phone list. When we tune in to our intuition, we're creating an open channel between ourselves and universal energy, and in order to make our "call" safely, we have to protect ourselves from any negative energy that might want to interfere.

We control spirits; they do not control us unless we give them the power to do so. Neither a living person nor a spirit has power over us unless we give it to him. Still, I insist that all my students are vigilant about protecting themselves, and you must do the same. No matter whether other energies are good, bad, or indifferent, you need to make sure you keep your own energy clear, clean, and safe. This is the only way to make sure the messages that you're getting are really accurate and for your benefit and are not designed to mislead or harm you.

There are several methods of protecting yourself when you use your intuition. First, imagine a white light surrounding you and whatever space you're in. If you have trouble imagining the light, think of yourself as a human lightbulb, radiating white light. The purity of white light will not only protect you but also, like a searchlight, will show any negative or trickster energies that might be trying to come in. Second, say a prayer of protection. Before every reading I say a prayer I've been using for almost twenty years. I've shared this prayer with my students, and many of them use it whenever they consciously tune in with their sixth sense:

> *We ask the Universal Consciousness*
> *that holds the highest spiritual power*
> *of Knowledge, Wisdom, and Truth*
> *to guide and protect us*
> *as we communicate with our guides*
> *and angels in the Spirit World*
> *and tap into the wisdom of the Universe.*
>
> *We respect this opportunity and*
> *take full responsibility to use this*
> *not for ego or controlling others*
> *but with the pure intention*
> *of spreading love and healing life*
> *on this earth and beyond.*

You're welcome to use my prayer or to adopt something from your own spiritual tradition. I know Catholics who say the rosary, Buddhists who chant mantras, and Native Americans who burn sage and perform a protection ritual before they tune in. Or if you prefer, just put the white light around you and ask for good energy to protect you. The key is your own intention to draw protection to yourself and keep negative energy away.

I always check any information I receive with the highest level of universal goodness. Spirits are like friends, and they can give you good and bad advice, so never take any information you receive without first checking it out. Ask for universal goodness to confirm your intuition and you're more likely to get accurate information.

Remember, energy never dies; it merely transmutes from one form to another. Develop a deep faith of knowing that you're protected and guided. Believe that there is an energy that flows through you, me, and everything. Believe that this energy is goodness and love. Believe that this energy can impart to you knowledge you can gain nowhere else. And believe that you can connect with that energy through your intuition.

Balance Is the Key

My sister Alicia is a wonderful psychologist, therapist, and family counselor. She's worked with children and parents for fifteen years, helping her clients get healthier psychologically, emotionally, and sometimes physically. We've worked together in several circumstances. Alicia sees daily how people are affected by the imbalances in their lives. "I think that sometimes we're afraid to let ourselves really listen," she says. "I think what gets in the way is always fear. Fear of the unknown, fear that we might be found out, fear that we might lose our comfort level even if it's not a healthy one. Because even though change is inevitable, people are afraid of it. Happily, we all have the power to heal ourselves, but the more positive thoughts and energy we bring to the situation, the more likely that healing will take place."

To find your own psychological, emotional, even physical balance, you have to be willing to face the truth. Learning to use your intuition entails learning the difference between true and false messages, between your desires and wishes and what the universe is offering you. Therefore, intuition requires that we be honest with ourselves. The only way to recognize real intuition is if we're willing to hear the truth and tell the truth. I see so many people who come for readings who are in massive denial about their own problems. They come hoping I will tell them what they want to hear, because they are living in fantasy instead of reality. You'd better believe I set them straight right away, or I tell them I won't read for them until they get therapy or clean up their act. How in the world can people expect the universe to show them the truth about one area of their lives if they're lying to themselves about their drinking, or their relationships, or their anger, or their spendthrift ways? We can all be in denial at different times. But to use your intuition with any accuracy, you'd better be honest about your strengths and weaknesses, your emotions and desires, the pretty parts and the not-so-pretty parts of your life.

Honesty is not just saying "Look at how many ways I'm messing up." It means recognizing your own greatness as well. It means having enough self-love to want to do what's best for you. It means not looking outside for love but finding it within you first. When you strive for this kind of honesty, it marks the end of wishful thinking, and it will become much easier for you to hear that intuitive voice.

Being honest also means being in touch with your own energy and striving for balance psychologically, emotionally, and physically. It's easy to allow yourself to get caught up in emotions, thoughts, and habits that throw you off balance. Maybe you had a bad day or a series of them. Maybe your kids aren't doing well in school and you're upset. Maybe you're a lifelong smoker and it's starting to affect the way you breathe. Sometimes even a cold can throw a person's intuitive sense off a little. When we're not balanced, we can become intuitively blind and lost. However, when we're balanced, we can be more perceptive and intuitive. We can recognize our own instincts, fears, and jealousies and not mistake them for signals from our sixth sense.

Our intuition involves every part of us: mind, body, and spirit. Our energy is housed in our bodies, channeled through our spirits, and interpreted by our minds. To be an effective and clear receiver for the universal signals of intuition, we've got to maintain a healthy balance. We have to understand our own energy and know what the proper balance is for us. We can't be messed up on drugs or alcohol, we can't be in abusive relationships, we can't allow ourselves to be constantly off-kilter in any way. If we want to connect with the highest energy of the universe, we must be able to attune ourselves to its vibrations, and that means we must keep ourselves as clear and balanced as possible.

This may sound like a lot of work just to use a sense that we already have! Perhaps. But isn't it to your benefit to clean up your act and tell the truth to yourself whether you're using your intuition or not? In truth, while intuition is our natural state, using it fully is a skill that requires preparation and practice. Tiger Woods was a good golfer who worked hard to become great. When Michael Jordan was a freshman in high school, he didn't even make the varsity team, but he worked hard and became one of the best basketball players in history. When we prepare to use our intuition, we are getting ready to put ourselves in touch with the greatest power in the universe. Doesn't that deserve a little time, honor, and respect?

3

Four Steps to Accessing
Your Inner Wisdom

Take a few moments now and make a list of all the times you received intuitive messages in your life. Start with childhood and continue to today. Did you know before anyone told you that you were going to have a little brother rather than a sister? Did you get a warning about someone's passing, or perhaps a loved one came to you in a dream? Then, for the next week, notice the moments of intuitive reception you're experiencing. Make notes of anything you think might be your intuition giving you a message. Maybe you just happen upon your passport, and the next day your boss tells you to plan for a trip out of the country. Notice coincidences, odd happenings, thoughts that don't seem to come from your conscious experience, feelings that lead you in a particular direction. Write down all of these incidents. They all probably won't be due to your intuition, but some of them will. And more important, you'll start recognizing the many ways the universe gives you intuitive messages.

I believe that attuning ourselves to intuitive messages is actually more essential than developing the skills to ask direct questions of our intuition. If the universe deems it important enough to send a message, we'd better be alert and ready to receive it! Its messages are often designed to warn us, help us prevent problems, or show us whether our path will lead to success or disaster. We can receive intuitive messages in almost every situation and circumstance, and for our health, safety, and happiness we need to recognize those messages when they appear. I usually suggest that people spend a year or more paying attention to the occurrences of intuitive reception that occur in their lives before they embark on any formal study of asking intuitively.

With intuitive asking, instead of the universe calling you, you're the one who's picking up your own "psychic cell phone" and making the call. It takes more effort, and you've got to be very attentive to discern the messages the universe provides in answer to your request. Intuitive reception can happen to anybody. It requires no belief in psychic abilities, no special training or circumstances. Intuitive asking is more demanding. While you can ask questions of the universe in any setting and at any time, you can learn to maximize the possibility of getting an accurate answer.

I teach intuitive asking in my workshops, and I've discovered there are specific things you can do to create a request that the universe can respond to, and then accurately interpret the reply. With intuitive asking, however, you need to remember that the future can change at any moment by anyone's decision or action. It's not all predestined, thank goodness; when we get an answer about something that might happen, many times we can step in and change the outcome. However, this also means that the answers we receive are not absolutely certain.

With either intuitive reception or intuitive asking, you need to be open-minded. Remember, our thoughts have enormous power. If you approach using your intuition with the thought "This will never work," guess what? You're probably right—if nothing else because you won't see the subtle signals intuition usually offers.

Here are the barriers you must overcome to access your God-given inner wisdom.

- *Overcome doubt and cultivate certainty.* Like everyone on earth, you *are* intuitive. Knowing this will open the door for your inner wisdom to come through.

- *Overcome caution and declare your desire.* As it says in the Bible, "Knock, and the door shall be opened."

- *Overcome selfishness and use your insights for the benefit of others as well as yourself.* We are given messages not only for our own sake, but also to help our fellow human beings.

- *Overcome self-delusion and face the truth about yourself.* If you're lying to yourself about your faults and problems, how can you expect your intuition to tell you the truth about anything else?

- *Overcome ego and cultivate gratitude.* Intuition is not about how great you are, but about tuning in to something much greater than yourself. Be grateful for the gift of guidance from universal wisdom.

- *Overcome arrogance and become a student again.* Developing your intuition will take practice and what Zen masters call "beginner's mind."

- *Overcome your fear of failure and be willing to make mistakes.* Accept the fact that you will be wrong sometimes. The only real mistake is not to try. Simply learn from your mistakes and move on.

- *Overcome your supposed limitations and push yourself.* You must go beyond what you think you can do. Keep asking questions about the information you're given until you feel a sense of clarity.

There are four steps for intuitive asking. I developed these steps over a long career of using and teaching intuition. I offer them for you to use and discover what works best for you. These powerful steps will allow you to manifest the life of abundance, fullness, and joy you desire, and to activate the power of the law of attraction in your life.

Step 1: Create the Right Atmosphere for Tuning In to the Universe

Intuitive asking requires your full attention. You want to make sure you can take a few minutes to really focus on your question or request. I suggest that if possible you go off by yourself, perhaps into another room. If you're a busy mom with little children running around, go in the bathroom and close the door. If you're working, close the door to your office and forward your calls if possible. Some people have a particular spot in their house where they sit. They light a candle or burn some incense. I suggest that you have a pen and paper handy, so you can capture any thoughts or impressions that might come up.

First, take a few deep breaths. Let yourself relax physically, mentally, and emotionally. Once you're comfortable and relaxed, close your eyes, put a white light around yourself, and say your prayer of protection to make sure that the energy replying to you comes from the highest level of universal energy. Use your prayer as another way of settling down and tuning in to a time, place, and energy that is separate from your everyday life.

Sometimes you can't take a quiet moment to yourself. Say you're driving in an unfamiliar town and you make a wrong turn into a bad neighborhood. You have no idea where you are, and there's no one in sight you would even consider asking for directions. In such cases, at a minimum you should take a deep breath and envelop yourself in a blinding white light before you move on to step 2.

Step 2: Focus on the Present and Clear Your Mind of Thoughts

Once you've said your prayer, bring yourself into the present moment. Some of you are probably thinking "How can I be anywhere else?" Well, have you ever known people who spent all their time in the past, remembering old relationships (good and bad), past traumas or victories, or even the great dinner they had last week? And how many of us spend an enormous amount of time in the future, dreaming of what might happen or worrying about possible problems? Great spiritual masters of all eras and countries tell us that enlightenment can be found if we just keep ourselves in the present moment by focusing the mind. This is also a great way to bring yourself out of daydreams and memories and back to what is. Being in the present moment will allow you to notice the messages you are receiving.

Another way to bring yourself into the present is simply to observe. Notice whatever is around you, without commenting on it or holding on to the thought. Notice how your body feels sitting in the chair, how your breath goes in and out, how the light hits the wall opposite you, the gentle whir of a heater or air conditioner. Do this for a minute or two and your mind will feel itself settling down and becoming clearer.

Once your mind is settled, clear your mind of thoughts. Imagine you're in a conversation with someone whom you trust completely because you know they have your best interests at heart. You're listening intently for their response to something you've said. You're not talking or forming an opinion; you're simply waiting to hear what they have to say. Try to forget about all that may be going on in your life. Bring yourself completely into the present. This is the most difficult step for most of us. Our brains are constantly filled with mind chatter: extraneous questions, impressions, thoughts, and emotions. With all that garbage, how is the universe going to hear our question, and how are we going to hear the reply?

The good news is that clearing your mind is definitely something that gets easier the more you practice it. Many people find that meditation is a great way to learn to clear their thoughts and empty their minds. Others find that focusing on something like a candle flame or a crystal or their breath or even a phrase is helpful. Or just use your mind to take yourself to a place where you feel peaceful—the beach, a forest, a mountain, a church, wherever your favorite place may be.

One of the best tools you can use to clear your mind is breath. Deep breathing cleans the body as well as the mind. Take a few deep breaths and then let your breathing return to normal. Focus on the breath for a while, then proceed with your meditation, visualization, or other focusing exercises.

To prepare to access your intuition you also need to clear out your emotions. Emotions, like thoughts, will get in the way of receiving the answer the universe has to give. Put your desires and wishes aside for a few moments. Let yourself be open to all possibilities. Think of this session as consulting with a very good friend. You need clarity and want an objective answer from someone you trust. Leave your emotions outside and come to your universal goodness with confidence that you will receive the answer you need. Connect with your personal highest energy of self-love and be your own best friend.

After I've cleared my mind, I close my eyes and focus my energy going out through the top of my head, toward the front. I also know I'm ready to ask my question and get an answer when I feel fully centered, balanced, and relaxed.

Step 3: Ask Your Question Without Being Emotionally Involved

Once you've cleared your mind of thoughts, ask your question. Try to make it as clear and concise as you can: "Am I supposed to take the job offer I received from XYZ Company yesterday?" "Should I move in with my boyfriend or girlfriend next month?" "Will my child do well at ABC Elementary School this year?" The questions don't have to have yes or no answers, but they must be very specific. The clearer your question, the easier it will be for you to discover and understand the answer the universe will offer (more about that in step 4).

Some people like to write down their question and then ask it. Of course, if you're in a situation where writing isn't practical or you don't have a lot of time, just ask your question in the best way you can and go with your gut response. For example, speed dating is a new way of meeting people. You go to a party and sit with potential dates for five minutes at a time. At the end of the evening you exchange numbers with anyone you want to see again. You can tell a lot about another person in five minutes, but he or she also may be very good at hiding the negative side of his or her nature. So I suggest that as each potential date sits down, clear your mind and ask the question, "Is this person a good match for me?" Then see what your first hit is.

Anytime you ask your question, you must make sure to be emotionally detached from the answer. (If you've focused your mind and put your emotions aside as described in step 2, this part will be easier.) Feeling peace and focused energy within yourself, ask your question with deep faith that you'll get the answer. Remember what I said in the last chapter about how desires and wishful thinking can get in the way of intuition. Put aside your desire for a specific answer to your question. If you're asking "Should I leave my partner?" and you're still deeply in love with him or her and don't want to leave, then you're not looking for an answer, you're looking for validation. And your desires will end up blocking the truth that your intuition is trying to tell you.

To create emotional distance, I've heard of people who

put their questions in the third person, as if they're asking for someone else. Bobby would ask, "Is Bobby going to leave his girlfriend?" or Sue would write, "Will Sue get this job?" You might try this if you find yourself getting emotional about the topic of your question. The main thing is to be objective when you ask your question, without emotional attachment to the answer, and with faith that the universe will tell you precisely what you need to know.

When I say *objective,* I don't mean skeptical. You're welcome to be skeptical about intuition and energy and everything else we're discussing, but not when you're trying to use intuitive asking. Skepticism not only will block your ability to ask a question objectively, but it also will prevent you from noticing the answers you might be given. It's like static on your psychic cell phone line—your question can't be heard and you can't understand the answer! Like any other emotion, you need to put your skepticism aside when you're asking a question of your intuition. Objective means neutral, neither believing nor disbelieving, just being absolutely clear in the moment and open to whatever may come through.

It's also possible that you're not supposed to receive an answer to your question at this moment. Much of our future is shaped by the choices we make, so the answer to your question may not be clear yet. Suppose you asked about moving in with your boyfriend or girlfriend, and you don't get an answer from your inner wisdom. And then the next week you're offered a great job with your company's branch in China. Your choice of whether or not to take the position definitely will affect your moving in with someone. The answer to your question also could depend on another person's decision. Suppose it isn't you but your boyfriend or girlfriend who gets the job offer—again, the answer to your question will change based on what they decide. Whenever you ask a question and there's no reply, you may need to trust that the answer will become clear as future events unfold.

Step 4: Pay Attention to What You're Getting

Once you've asked your question, keep your mind clear and pay attention to what comes up for you. Stay objective and trust the first thought that comes into your head. This answer is different from a thought you think; it's a thought given to you, one that flows in from another place in your mind. Many of us have a sense of exactly where our conscious thoughts arise in our minds. But have you ever had something—a thought, an impression, a "knowing"—pop into your head and then immediately think, *Wherever did* that *come from?* Psychic thoughts or intuitions can feel like they appear from nowhere, because they arise from a part of the brain other than the place where our conscious thoughts appear. For example, when I read for people, I focus my attention on the front of my brain, high up toward my forehead. That's where messages seem to pop into my head that have nothing to do with my conscious mind and everything to do with the person I'm reading for.

Psychic thoughts or impressions also can come through other areas of the body. Your answer could take the form of a gut feeling, goose bumps, or perhaps a chill down your back. Often we just know our intuitive answers are true because they have a particular sensation attached to them, a sense of "Yep, that's it," whether it's the answer that we wanted to hear or not. After I've asked my question, I focus my energy toward the front of my head and wait until a thought comes to me that is the answer to my question. The thought that doesn't come from my own mind is the answer I am seeking.

Some people like to write down what's coming to them. They put pen to paper and write everything that comes up—thoughts, feelings, emotions, and sensations. For them it's a great way to capture the answers freely, without letting the conscious, logical brain edit their impressions. Then later they can review the information and see what feels right.

Many people feel far from clear when their intuition flashes. Usually they're confused and want to shrug off the experience. For instance, they're thinking of someone who has passed over and just then the lights flicker for no apparent reason and they say, "I must have imagined it." Or they turn immediately to a left-brain-based, logical interpretation—perhaps a short-circuit in the lamp (never mind that there's never been a problem with that lamp before, and there's no problem with it other than that one instance). Have you ever felt intuitively that someone is lying to you, but you shrug it off, only to find out later you were right? It's very important not to negate our intuitive impulses when they arise. When you've asked an intuitive question, believe that your answer may come in many different ways, and don't edit or try to explain. Interpretation can come later; for now you want simply to notice what you're getting. Even if it seems that on the surface a thought doesn't have any relation to your question, the universe might be telling you exactly what you need to know.

For example, you might ask the question "Is my sister going to buy a new house?" and your answer may be, "When she does buy a house, it's going to be out of state." The answer you get may be different from your original question, but perhaps your sister didn't tell you that she was up for a job in another state. The answer you received was more important than your specific question (and if she takes the job she'll probably have to buy a new house anyway). But it may not be the direct answer. Or perhaps you ask, "Is my boyfriend going to leave me?" and all of a sudden Mary's face pops into your head, and you get the feeling that maybe your boyfriend's seeing Mary on the side. If that's the case, it's almost as if he's already left you, isn't it? And would you really want to stay with him anymore?

Your answer also may take a form other than a thought or a feeling. It might be something you see or hear or all of a sudden become aware of. If you ask, "How am I going to do on my performance review at work?" you might open your eyes and see today's mail. On the top of the pile is an advertisement for an automobile, and the headline reads SUPERSTAR-RATED! There's your answer in black and white! When you've asked a question of your inner wisdom, often you'll find that things you might have called "chance" and "coincidence" are really the universe finding a different way to provide your answer.

If you're in one of those situations where you need an answer right away, as soon as you ask your question pay careful attention to every subtle cue in your environment. What's your first thought or feeling? Is there something in your environment that might be giving you a sign—something you see or hear? I read one story of a man who was looking for a country club in a rural area. He asked the intuitive question, "Which way should I go?" A moment later, he turned on the radio and heard, "Don't forget: turn left at the railroad crossing!" He looked up and, sure enough, there was a railroad crossing a little way down the road. He took the left-hand turn and made it safely to the country club.

Another client was driving down a strange road and wanted to stop and ask for directions, but she was in a bad part of town. She asked her intuition for guidance, then turned to her young son who was in the car with her and said, "We need to stop and ask for directions. What do you think about that gas station?" He immediately said, "No—there are bad men there." They drove a little farther and came upon another gas station. The woman asked her son for advice again, and this time he said, "That one's fine, Mom." Did she ever know truly that she would have been attacked if she had stopped at the first gas station? Of course not. But I believe in the old motto "Better safe than sorry." I'd rather listen to a child's intuition and drive a little farther than ignore it and possibly put myself and my child into harm's way.

Above all, be patient. Often our intuitive messages come at different times in the day or night, when our conscious minds are less active and we're more open to the promptings of our intuition. You might find that you'll get answers to your questions right before you fall asleep. Or you'll wake up at three in the morning and all of a sudden the answer appears. Or you might receive the answer in a dream. The few minutes after you wake up from a nap or in the morning are prime times for intuitive answers because these are times when the conscious mind is disengaged and less likely to negate what we receive. You also should give yourself a day or two for the answer to appear. Sometimes your answer will come later in the day or week or month, but you'll know when it hits you!

*   *   *

Intuition isn't infallible. You can interpret what your intuition brings you and be wrong—but you also may be right. When you're in sync with your own energy and know right from wrong from within, you can trust your instincts. There's a special "feeling" that occurs when an answer feels right. It's something that each of us experiences in a different way. Some people feel the hair on their arms standing up or get goose bumps. Others just have a sense of balance. Whatever the answer, you will feel complete, as if you just put in the last piece of a puzzle. Whether the answer is your desire or not, when you are honest about your thoughts and feelings the truth will jump out at you.

What If the Answer Doesn't Come Right Away, or At All?

You can't ask your question and then force the universe to answer it through your willpower. Just like when you are manifesting, for example, asking for a new Mercedes within twenty-four hours, it may or may not happen depending on a lot of factors, including your state of mind. If you're having a problem getting an answer, or you think that you're making up an answer because it's what you want, you may still be too emotionally attached or your mind isn't cleared. Do you remember the old expression "A watched pot never boils"? Get some distance from your question. If you're too close to it and yet you really need an answer, you can say to your intuition, "Okay, I'm too close to this. Please in the next week show me some kind of a sign." Give yourself some space and time away from it, and the universe may very well bring you an answer—or that Mercedes—faster than you realize.

In these circumstances, often the answer comes when you least expect it. Say your question was "Will I be ready if my boss gives me that big new job?" You asked it and got nothing that felt like an answer to you. But it's something you're thinking about so constantly that you have no distance. So you release your question and go about your day. You may wake up in the middle of the night thinking, "I need to clear up three current projects if I'm going to even be able to take on the new job." Or maybe the next day you call a friend who is at the same stage of his career who mentions he's just accepted the same kind of position. Or you might get an e-mail from your sister saying, "John, you've always gotten what you really went after," and you get goose bumps. (I call those "Oh my gosh" moments, where you understand that you've received your answer.) You say to yourself, "I'm going to be ready for this job when my boss offers it to me." The answer to your question may come in many forms and in its own time.

You also may have to wait for the answer because things are still in flux around this particular issue. There isn't always a definitive answer to every question, because other people's actions and decisions may be influencing the outcome. Suppose you ask whether you will be given a certain contract for your business, and you don't get any kind of hit one way or another. You find out later that the company has just gone through a massive reorganization, and all outside contracts have been put on hold for three months. You still may get the job, but nothing's going to be decided for the next ninety days. In such cases, no answer *is* your answer, and you have to rely on your logic and common sense to give you direction until things settle down.

Take Action on What the
Universe Is Giving You

Once you've used your intuition to get an answer, you must decide what action you want to take as a result. We are partners with the universe: it's giving us the guidance, but we have to do something with what we're given. We're the ones who are in control of our destiny—as Hamlet said, "The fault lies not in our stars, but in ourselves." Although some things in life are predestined, we create most of our path in life. If you ask whether you should leave your lover and the universe comes back with a strong "Yes!" and you decide to stay anyway, don't be surprised if it ends badly.

Using intuition to help guide us isn't abdicating our responsibility for our choices in life. In fact, I think it takes us to a higher level of responsibility because we are reaching beyond our own desires and wishes and asking for guidance from a higher place so that we can be in alignment with the universal plan. To use your intuition as a guide in life, I believe you need the four C's:

1. *Courage.* It takes guts to see beyond your own desires and take action based on a bigger plan. You also need to have the courage to face the truth and the courage to make mistakes.

2. *Confidence.* You must believe in yourself and your intuitive insights, and you must be confident that you can carry out what the universe guides you to do.

3. *Commitment.* You must be committed to developing your intuition and to partnering with your inner wisdom in creating your destiny. And you should have enough commitment to be patient with yourself as you're learning.

4. *Conquer.* You must conquer your own thoughts, your fears, your skepticism, and the doubts of others. You must triumph over any desire to hold on to what isn't in alignment with your inner voice. Once you conquer these negative tendencies, you will succeed.

Now it's up to you. To develop intuitive asking takes practice. Like a muscle, the more you use it the stronger your sixth sense gets. You'll also learn more about your own intuitive style, and you'll be able to more readily pick up on the cues the universe is offering you. In the same way that an artist knows more about color and form than the average person, or a musician knows more about sound, and a chef can discern more flavors in a dish, with practice you'll be able to draw more information and guidance from your intuition. When that happens, you may discover that your choices in life become, if not easier, at least clearer. More important, you will know how to stay in sync with the guidance of the universal energy that runs through us all.

4

Making Your Wisest Choices

The intuitive mind is a sacred gift and the rational mind is a faithful servant. We have created a society that honors the servant and has forgotten the gift.

—Albert Einstein

I once came upon a very charismatic gentleman who was eating lunch in the food court of a mall. Immediately I picked up that the spirit of an older woman, Janet, who was with him, and he confirmed that it was his great-grandmother. Before Janet died, she had said she would be with him always and would watch over the family through him. Then he told me that he had been trying to make a very difficult decision to tell the truth about something to certain people in his life. He hadn't even been able to sleep the night before. But because I had reminded him of his great-grandmother and her invisible presence, he knew what he had to do.

Almost every day of our lives we're faced with easy and difficult choices. This road or that one? Take the phone call or let it go to voice mail? Go on the date or avoid this person like the plague? Take the job or keep looking? Break off the relationship or work on it? If you're like me, you were taught to use common sense for the small choices—to ask, "What road makes the most sense?" For the bigger choices, in your career or relationship, for example, you'd use the logical, thinking part of your brain to evaluate the pros and cons of each side and then make the most rational choice. But I believe that making decisions only based on logic or common sense is missing out on one of the most basic sources of information: your intuitive, wiser self. Like my friend in the food court, tapping into your intuition can help you make the best choice and give you greater peace of mind with the decision you make.

Here's a small example of intuition, common sense, and logic in very practical terms. One Friday a good friend of mine called, distraught. He had lost his dog and asked me to help find her. The first thing we did was to spend Saturday looking in all the places we thought the dog could be (common sense). We also searched the area where someone had reported seeing the dog, even though it was miles away from where the dog was lost (common sense again). Then we looked in the places where the dog might have gone, assuming she could only run so far in that amount of time (logic). No dog. Well, Sunday morning I woke up at about 7 A.M. and immediately called my friend. "Leave right now, go exactly where we were last night, take your other dog with you so she'll have a familiar energy around her, and you'll find your dog," I said. In that moment the energy was so strong that I knew the timing had to be right. He went to the area where we had been searching and there was his dog, safe and sound. My intuition had provided the final piece of the puzzle that logic and common sense had failed to solve. (Of course, as a spiritual intuitive I might have had an edge, but we're all capable of using our intuition in such cases.)

Many people recognize the value of intuition in making good choices, only they don't call it "intuition." Instead, you'll hear terms like *gut check*, or *that feels right*, or they'll get a *hit* on something. All these words describe knowing without knowing how we know—getting information from a place other than the conscious part of the brain. We all have this ability, yet in most modern "civilized" circumstances we've been taught that intuitive feelings aren't a valid source of information. Intuition has been denigrated as being inferior to logic and common sense—until recently. Today many business and personal development books are starting to talk about the benefits of intuition when it comes to decision making. There even have been studies showing that people who make decisions based on analysis are *less* satisfied than those who rely on gut feelings to make their choices. Soldiers training to go into battle are taught to trust their instincts (e.g., their intuitive sense of danger) along with common sense and logic when it comes to keeping themselves safe.

I need to make something very clear when it comes to the term *intuition*. Many popular books define intuition as something we develop as a result of our experience. We build up references in a particular field—as a firefighter, for instance—about what to do in certain situations. We go into so many burning buildings, see how fire acts in so many different ways, and we learn what to do so well that it becomes automatic, almost unconscious. We can see signs of danger before anyone else with less experience. Instead of needing to analyze consciously what's happening with a fire, we immediately know what to do because we've seen it before.

Certainly our past experiences can make us more sensitive to the currents of energy in that particular area. It's like being in a relationship for a long time; you can become more intuitively attuned with your spouse or child and be more sensitive to what's going on with them even if they're not in your presence. And certainly most people in work situations become far more attuned to reading the energy in the atmosphere of the workplace, whether anything is overtly communicated or not. But a firefighter with past references and good experience-based intuition can still get hurt, while his rookie colleague in the same situation has an intuitive sense of danger and does what it takes to escape unharmed.

Intuition is not confined to bringing up information that's stored in our subconscious. As millions of people will attest, intuition puts us in touch with information that is completely outside our own experience, drawn from far wider knowledge—part of the energy of life itself. We can use this greater source of information to help us make better choices even when we have no experience or references. And when we combine information and inspiration, logic, common sense, and universal knowledge, we find our wisest answers.

I'm not saying that you should always follow your gut any more than I'm saying you should always follow your logic and common sense. You shouldn't walk the streets of a bad neighborhood at midnight saying, "My intuition will tip me off if there's danger" and think that that's all the protection you need. I believe that logic and common sense are absolutely vital when it comes to guiding our lives. If intuition is our sixth sense, God also gave us a seventh—common sense! I'm not interested in people who say they let their intuition guide them no matter what it tells them. These are the kinds of people who will give all their money to fake psychics and con men. Such people can be a danger to themselves and to others. You're not God, and your intuition is not infallible. There are also negative and trickster energies that can give you false messages. That's why one of the most important functions of our logic and common sense is to provide a second and third checkpoint for any intuitive direction we may receive.

On the other hand, I also think that people who use only logic and common sense are missing out on a vital source of information and guidance. Taking a few moments to listen to the inner wisdom of your intuition will help you make better, wiser choices than if you rely on logic and common sense alone. Intuition can help you get past the roadblocks of fear and caution that keep you from learning and growing. Indeed, intuition can take you places logic and common sense never could.

Using Intuition, Common Sense, and Logic to Decide Wisely

Whenever you're faced with a big decision, it's important to evaluate it using intuition, common sense, and logic. I tend to start with intuition: what's my first impression about this particular situation? Let's use a business example. You're offered a chance to participate in a team working on a new project. It will mean more hours but could be very good for your career if it goes well. What's your first hit when the project comes to you? Do you feel excited? Nervous? Is there something that says "Yes!" inside you, or perhaps a feeling of impending disaster? Maybe you get an unbidden thought, "If David's involved with this, it will be sure to succeed." Pay attention to your first impression about this opportunity.

Now you can apply common sense. Common sense tells you this project is a great opportunity, one that might not come along again anytime in the near future. (Or perhaps common sense tells you that you already have way too much on your plate and you can't take on anything else, or maybe you have a family vacation planned in the near future and you can't change the dates.) I consider common sense a great "first pass" for the conscious part of the brain. Common sense looks at the big picture and gives you its vote, up or down. Once you've taken a look at the big picture, you can apply the more detailed analysis of logic. Make a list of pros and cons; analyze the benefits and drawbacks of taking on the project or not. This will satisfy the conscious mind's need for validation and input while perhaps providing you with greater clarity.

However, once you've done all that, I suggest you go back to your intuition. Remember, intuition is tapping into two extremely valuable sources of wisdom. First, it is your access to the information stored in your subconscious mind. The subconscious is capable of discerning far more than we can access consciously. It's where we make instantaneous connections between seemingly unrelated pieces of information. It's where our emotions and our intellect meet input from sources outside ourselves. Your subconscious mind may tell you that there are potential problems with certain team members, or perhaps you get a sense that there's a lot of support for this project from the executive team. (Later you remember hearing a company vice president saying that the company's looking to go in a new direction, and this project is in complete alignment with that plan. You didn't store that memory consciously, but your subconscious used it to give you a feeling of confidence.) Again, ask yourself, "With all the analysis I've done, how do I *feel* about each choice?"

Finally, use your intuition again to tap into a source of wisdom beyond your conscious and subconscious mind. Use the steps that I described earlier for intuitive asking. Intuition can read the subtle currents of universal energy that surround your decision. Your intuition may be able to pick up on potential hazards and conflicts that you can't know about, or show you that this project is the golden door that will take you to an entirely new level of success. Make sure you leave behind your logic, common sense, and the desires and wishes of your subconscious, and go straight to that highest level of wisdom. That's the best place to get the final word on what you should do.

How Fear Can Be Your Friend or Your Foe

One of the main ways our intuition tips us off is through fear. Sometimes it's a twinge of discomfort or a feeling of something not being right. This can be your intuitive sense warning you about a situation that hasn't reached your conscious mind yet. Maybe you go to make the same trip to the grocery store you've made hundreds of times before, only today you feel uneasy as soon as you get in the car. Something feels strange; you can't put your finger on it, there isn't a specific noise or wiggle that you're noticing, but your sixth sense is warning you that something's amiss with your car. You drive to the local mechanic instead of the grocery store and find that one of your tires has a nail in it, and if you'd driven very far it could have blown out and caused an accident.

Other times you'll be certain that there is imminent danger and you need to get out *now*. You walk down a street and notice a man following you at a distance. You can't see him clearly but your intuition starts screaming, "Get away from him!" You go into the first store you come to and ask one of the sales clerks to walk you out to your car. You turn on the TV news that evening and see the man's face: he was involved in a carjacking just a few streets away from where you spotted him. When we get those strong, specific intuitive warnings, we ignore them at our peril, because they are designed to keep us safe from harm.

However, in other circumstances fear can actually keep us from using our intuition. Fear can be a friend to warn us about something, yet living in constant fear stops us from living life fully. You might not sense when the universe is trying to warn you about something because the fear is creating too much psychic "noise." And if you're afraid that the signals you're getting from the universe are "supernatural" or not in your best interests, you're going to stop tuning in. That's not to say that fear is bad; it's actually one of the key ways the universe tips us off to potential problems or negative energies. But you've got to check out your fear to make sure it's a valid response to your situation.

So how do you know whether the fear you're feeling is valid or just your mind and emotions getting in the way? This is one of the best places to put your logic and common sense to work. What's triggering the fear? It could be a common-sense response to the large, scowling man who's staring at you from across the street. And it may be logical to be a little afraid when you take your first scuba dive or your first tandem jump from an airplane, or to be nervous when your child goes off to school for the first time. But are those fears appropriate given your circumstances, and do you need to take action on them? That's when you should evaluate using your logic and common sense. If there's no reason for the fear other than the fact that you're facing a new and challenging experience or you're a habitual worrier who's scared of everything or you're uncertain as to what the outcome of the experience will be, then I suggest you ask your logic and common sense, "What's really going on here?" Then put a white light of protection around yourself and perhaps say a prayer, to ensure you're insulated should you be picking up on negative energies that do not wish you well. Once you've done that, reevaluate your situation and see if you want to proceed or wait or leave the circumstances entirely.

I also suggest doing a gut check to see if this is a logical fear or an intuitive warning. Most of us can tell when we have a "Get out!" response when faced with a situation. It's almost as if our survival instinct is kicking in. In such cases, I strongly suggest following your gut and taking some action that will help you get rid of the fear or get out of the situation.

Knowing yourself is an important component of deciding whether fear is a clear signal or mental static. Is fear your usual response to most situations? Does fear cause you to become unresourceful or to freeze up, or does it cause you to take action? Do you feel fear centered on specific people or situations, perhaps due to incidents in your past? If you've been mugged or assaulted or abused, it wouldn't be surprising for you to fear walking down dark streets or dating a person who reminds you of your ex. Are you afraid of harm coming to your loved ones, especially your children? Do you have fears about work, about being accepted, about performing below your own standards or the standards of other people? Are you afraid for your physical safety, and does it keep you from taking part in activities like diving, flying, or running? When it comes to analyzing fear, "Know thyself" is one of the first commandments. Only when you know your own psychological makeup can you decide if fear is coming from inside your own mind or is a signal of warning from the universe.

The antidote to fear is a combination of preparation and faith. Use your common sense and logic to prepare yourself to handle the situations that your fear might warn you about. You can also prepare by always throwing a white light of protection around yourself whenever you feel the least twinge of fear. But once you've prepared, you need to have faith that the universe will tip you off to what you need to know. When you live with faith and a positive attitude, any intuitive warnings will come in much more clearly, and all you have to do is to pay careful attention. Because intuition is designed to tip you off when you truly need to be warned, it can help you get past the roadblocks of fear and caution that keep you from learning and growing. When you use your intuition properly, fear can become a valuable servant rather than a demanding master.

What If Intuition Goes One Way and Logic Another?

I recently read an account of a woman who was looking for work for quite a while. Finally she accepted a great job about an hour away from her home. She was required to do two weeks of training with the company before she started her position. The job was great, but she was having some problems with the two-hour commute. Toward the end of her training, she was driving home and a thought flashed into her head: *This isn't going to work.* She hadn't been evaluating her job, she wasn't weighing the pros and cons, but she just *knew* in that moment this job wasn't right for her. It took courage, but she went in and resigned the next day. Sure, she had manifested a job. Sure, it was what she needed and wanted. But she'd left out some important details—like distance from her home.

When we first start to listen to intuition and listen to it showing us how to manifest the desires of our heart, it's sort of like Luke Skywalker in *Star Wars* holding the light saber for the first time. The power is unwieldy, it's huge, it's uncontrollable. And it is precisely at that moment you can be joyful that you have found it at all. The ability to listen to your heart, to verbalize your deepest desire, to grow into your power, and then to manifest only that which serves your highest good and that of all concerned—this is the truest application of your intuition.

Whenever you're faced with a choice, if logic, common sense, and intuition are all pointing you in the same direction, you can pretty much assume it's the right way to go. Those are the easy choices. But what if logic and common sense are pointing one way and yet your intuition, your gut, isn't going along? Sometimes we discount or ignore those very clear messages or *aha's* of our intuition. That's when our logic and common sense can actually work against us. We start thinking, "It doesn't make any sense to leave this job, I've only been there for two weeks," even though our intuition is saying,

"This isn't going to work." But making a decision while ignoring the promptings of intuition is like driving down a road and not paying attention to the flashing sign on the shoulder saying BRIDGE WASHED OUT—DETOUR AHEAD. It can lead you into more trouble than you want or need.

Have you ever wanted something—maybe it was a romantic relationship or a business deal—and on paper it looked good, but you had a gut feeling that it wasn't right? Then you did it anyway and suffered the consequences? On the other hand, perhaps you followed that gut feeling that went against all logic, and it led to a successful result. These are the toughest choices. These are the ones that require the four C's I talked about in chapter 3: courage, confidence, commitment, and the ability to conquer your own fears and overcome the resistance of others. Great leaders in all walks of life, from Winston Churchill, Mahatma Gandhi, Mother Teresa, and Nelson Mandela to Lee Iacocca, Donald Trump, and Walt Disney have defied logic and common sense to pursue their dreams and visions. And where do our dreams and visions come from if not our intuitive connection with something far greater than ourselves?

Intuition is just as important as logic and common sense, because those intuitive flashes can keep you safe, prepare you, and perhaps point you in a different direction. If after you've evaluated a situation using the process I describe in chapter 3, and you find logic and common sense are telling you one thing and your intuition is telling you another, I would suggest following your intuition. Carefully, though—you must keep checking with your intuition to see if the choices you're making continue to feel right. When the truth is there, you will have a feeling of just knowing from deep in your soul. Keep checking with that highest level of wisdom, and eventually one of two things will happen: your intuition will be proved right, or you'll discover that perhaps you have made a mistake in interpreting what your intuition had to say. There are times when people feel they shouldn't get on a plane because it is going to crash, and the plane lands at its destination safely. There are other times when people follow their intuition and take a job or get into a relationship and it ends up badly. Intuition isn't infallible—but then, neither are logic and common sense. The main thing is to make the best of whatever situation you're in. Make choices with a clear conscience, knowing that intuition leads us to make the choices that ultimately are for our greatest good, so following its lead will be to your benefit.

Roadblocks May Be Blessings in Disguise

Okay, you've made your decision based on logic, common sense, and intuition, you've started to take action in that direction—and you run smack dab into a roadblock. You've decided someone is the man or woman of your dreams; you ask him or her out only to be turned down. You put in your bid to work on a particular project, only to be told the team is full. You choose a course in school, but you can't come up with the money for your tuition in time to enroll for the fall. It sometimes seems that the universe delights in pointing us in a certain direction and then putting up barriers that keep us from making the progress we want.

When we make a choice that we feel is aligned with intuition, logic, and common sense only to discover that things don't work out in the way we hope or expect, the barriers we encounter may be protecting us from unwanted consequences of our decision. The team at work may be fated to fall apart. Maybe the man of your dreams is just getting over a bad relationship and he would be dating you for the wrong reasons, which you'd discover too late. Maybe you're meant to take your classes at a different school. Your decision may be right but the time and circumstances that will make it right haven't come together yet, and you may need to develop patience. Universal wisdom isn't tied to any kind of timetable, because time has very little meaning at the level of universal goodness and love. It's quite possible to pick up on intuitive information that will be valid in your future rather than now. If the choice you made based on that intuition doesn't pan out, just file your impressions away and see if your intuitive hit comes true at a later date.

Sometimes we make a decision based on common sense, logic, and intuition and then things shift in the universe. Hard to believe, but there are others who can affect the situations of your life! As Carol Adrienne points out in *The Purpose of Your Life,* there are many complex factors in any situation we may encounter. You may have checked logic, common sense, and intuition when you planned a great vacation on the beaches of Thailand in January 2005, but then the tsunami hit in December 2004 and your perfect beach was decimated. Forces far beyond your control have changed your plans. Or you planned your vacation and all of a sudden your husband's intuition about getting a new job comes true, and you have to postpone your trip. In any situation, other people and other forces can change the outcome after we've reached our conclusion. In those cases, go back to your logic, common sense, and intuition and see what your next step should be.

It's even possible that your destiny is to make a wrong

choice. You may have karma that needs to play itself out with a person or situation. (As we'll discuss in chapter 6, many of our relationships exist to help us learn and grow and reach the next level in our development.) Or the partner we choose may be there not because the relationship is going to work out, but because there's a connection from a past life that needs to play out. It's also possible that this is a relationship we need to go through because we have unresolved issues with love and commitment, and we need to work out those issues before we can find the relationship we truly want.

Often we make wrong decisions because we need to learn the lessons for our greater good. Haven't you made a wrong choice in your life that, while possibly painful, taught you a valuable lesson? Most of life's experiences happen for a reason: to teach us lessons, both easy and hard. Most of us are all for lessons and signs from the universe, but we just want the pleasant lessons and the nice signs. "Lord, show me a sign that this is the right school for my child!" But then the next thing you know, your child is kicked out of school for fighting, and it turns out he has a learning disorder that's causing him to act out. You would never have known that if he hadn't messed up in school.

It's unfortunate but true that we learn a lot more from a painful experience than a pleasurable one. We've got to be willing to tune in and learn the lessons before we can move on. If part of your lesson is to keep pursuing this boyfriend until he blatantly cheats on you, then that may be the way you have to learn. Just make sure you never waste the lessons the universe brings your way. Learn from them the first time; otherwise, you may encounter the same lessons again and again until you get them down pat. One of the reasons to use your intuition, logic, and common sense is to be able to learn your lessons quickly and then move on.

Suppose you consulted your inner wisdom and you're still not clear. It could be you're just not meant to know about this particular area. There may be something new and different that you're supposed to learn, and not being able to tune in is an element of the learning process. While this may be frustrating, quite honestly, wouldn't it be awful never to be surprised? To know everything that the universe has in store for us? We can't know everything anyway, because we make our own destiny and not everything is written in stone. But I believe part of our lesson for being on earth is to learn to take a chance, to risk, to leap without knowing what awaits us. We must put 100 percent of ourselves into life, and if it's meant to be, then it will happen in its own time, or in God's time. We're just responsible for making the leap.

Remember, it's not about predicting the future but about the choices we make along the way. Different paths can lead to the same destination. Learn to accept uncertainty. Acceptance of a situation you can't control at the moment is a wise trait to develop.

The Power of Our Intention

Once you've made a decision that's in tune with your intuition and supported by common sense and logic, you will have to put that decision into tangible form. We talked a little bit in a previous chapter about putting our intuitions into action, but there is an aspect of action that is far beyond the efforts of our hands. Thoughts are deeds: they are so powerful that creating an image in your mind can produce enormous energy, a subconscious reality that has infinite potential. Once we put our thoughts out there, they have life: in essence, you might as well consider a thought the same as an act. We take action through the power of our thoughts and our intention. There is no more important force in the world than aligning our thoughts and intentions with the guidance we receive from our universal connection.

Through *The Secret,* a lot of people today are learning what I've known for a long time: the power of intention to attract what they want into their lives. Intention is where thought and intuition join hands with universal energy. Intention puts the power of both conscious and subconscious mind behind our pure desire and links it to the world and universe outside ourselves.

When we will things into our lives, however, our intent must be strong and direct. You have to know that you deserve it. If you have the slightest doubt that you don't deserve something, it will stop the creative flow of its birth. You must put the thought out in the ethers with confidence, then let it happen. Remember that you have to release the desire and the thought. Don't dwell on it, but every so often give it a thought. That gives the universe a chance to do its work, for the eddies and currents of energy to align themselves to support your intention.

After a number of experiments, one scientist who conducted research on the power of intention tried to use intention himself to achieve certain outcomes. He found out that in his own case, trying to force his will on the universe just didn't work—he described it as trying to will himself to sleep. Setting the intention and then letting go, or pursuing it with what he called "gentle energy," produced better results. And as he was able to achieve more and more outcomes, he quickly became known in his laboratory as a "very good wisher."

Intention and the power of our thoughts are some of the most important forces we can harness. But I also believe that we must always call upon the other two aspects of inner wisdom—logic and common sense—in creating the lives we desire. You may put out the intention and the thought "I have perfect teeth," but you'd better also get to the dentist on a regular basis to make sure you get good quality dental care. You may attract lots of money or even find the perfect financial advisor through your intention, but you still should use common sense and logic when you choose your investments and keep track of your results. Intention and thought taps us into the power of universal energy, but the universe darned well expects us to put in the work when it comes to manifesting what we want to have in our lives!

For at least two hundred years most Western countries have focused on logic, common sense, and hard work as the only means for people to create happy, successful lives. What I find exciting is that for the first time people are starting to understand the power of intention and intuition, when combined with logic and common sense, to help us find our way, discover our true desires, and live in tune with what the universe wants for us. We each have a path that we are supposed to tread, but how we walk it and how easy it is largely is within our control. By using all our powers—logic, common sense, intuition, intention, and action—we find our journey on this earth to be more fulfilling and our lessons more rewarding. When we do so, we are living in alignment with our deepest desires, which lead us to learn, grow, and love.

In the rest of this book, we're going to be talking a lot about the power of following both intention and intuition in directing the course of our lives in relationships, health, career, sex, finances, and parenting. I hope it will be eye-opening as you learn how you can use your intuition and connection to the universe to draw more of what you want into your life and banish what you don't.

One warning, however: be careful what you ask for, because you might just get it. The universe works by specific laws, and sometimes we can use the power of attraction and intention to manifest people, work, possessions, or events that are not in our best interests. We can delude ourselves that what we wish for is what the universe wants for us. In such cases, eventually we'll discover that perhaps our desires and intention drowned out the real voice of our inner wisdom, and we need to learn our lesson and move on. Before you ever activate the law of attraction, always take the time to consult your inner wisdom. It will always have your best interests at heart, and it will keep you aligned with what the universe wishes to offer to you for your highest good. Remember, accessing your inner wisdom isn't simply tuning in to what the universe may have in store for you; it's actively using your inner wisdom to create a better, happier life.

5

Your Inner Wisdom and Health

The wish for healing has ever been the half of health.

—Seneca, *Hippolytus*

About three years ago, my sister Alicia's husband, Paul, had just seen a new cardiologist, who had reviewed Paul's medications and put him on a different regimen. Paul began taking the new prescriptions over a weekend. On Sunday night, however, I started feeling something was wrong. I called Alicia and said, "I'm worried that Paul's going to have a major heart attack. There's something wrong with his medication." Alicia explained the new regimen and laughed at me a little. "Paul feels great; you're wrong this time," she said. But I knew different. "You have to call Dr. Brownstein right now," I insisted. "I don't care if it's nine-thirty on a Sunday night—get him on the phone."

Alicia agreed to call Dr. Brownstein, who is a great doctor and alternative medicine practitioner as well as an expert on natural hormones. Dr. Brownstein knows my work and knows I wouldn't insist on Alicia calling unless it was serious. He told her, "I'll meet you in my office right now if you and Char feel it's necessary." They agreed that since Paul felt fine the visit could wait until the morning. At 8 A.M. Alicia and Paul were in Dr. Brownstein's office. Paul had brought all his medications with him, and Dr. Brownstein looked them over. Then he stopped and held up one bottle. "Where did you get this thyroid prescription?" he said. "It's triple the amount you're supposed to take." Somewhere along the line there had been a mistake in filling the thyroid prescription. The triple level of thyroid medication was speeding up Paul's heart, which easily could have resulted in a heart attack.

Most of us have had the experience of "knowing" something's wrong with us physically long before obvious symptoms appear. Sometimes we're warned about problems; sometimes, as in Paul's case, we're not. In this situation, I was the one who picked up on the signals from the universe and got Paul the help he needed. It could just as easily have been Alicia who sensed something was wrong, or Paul himself. I firmly believe that all of us have the ability to tune in to our health when we pay attention to it, to prevent problems both big and small.

In high school science class you probably learned that our bodies are made up of atoms, which combine to make molecules, which combine to make matter, which composes the tissue, blood, muscles, and so on. But without energy, all of these bits of matter are lifeless. There is an energy that enlivens the human body that is the same energy that runs the universe. Health is an expression of the energy of the body. In the same way we can use our intuition to bring us information that we couldn't know consciously, we can use our intuition to connect us to the energy currents within the body. When we use our intuition in relation to our physical health, we can sense when our energy—our life force—is flowing freely and well, or when it's being impeded by fatigue, poor diet, stress, or disease. Intuition is our means of tuning in to truths about our health that the conscious mind cannot know or is denying.

We tune in to this energy all the time when we use our intuition. When we hear or feel something that is psychic we often get goose bumps. Goose bumps are a sign from the body that means the truth is being spoken. Some people feel a definite chill. These are just a few examples of the power of energy and intuition to affect the body. There are medical intuitives who specialize in reading the physical energy of their clients and helping them get to the root of disease and/or make healthier choices for their lives. While I am not a medical intuitive and I don't diagnose or prescribe, I do pick up on health issues in my readings. I can tell if someone is having a potential problem with a particular area of the body. When I'm on a television show and giving readings over the phone, I'll ask a caller, "Are you having problems with your foot? Go see your doctor." In one reading, a man named Max came through very strongly to speak to his grandson, Wilson. "Max wants you to know that he's watching over the family," I said. "Edith, his daughter—is she having any problem with her feet or legs?"

"Her knees," the grandson replied.

"Well, she may need a cane for walking, and Max says to tell her not to be vain and use it," I told him.

You don't have to be highly attuned or a medical intuitive to know that your energy, or the energy of someone else, is "off." Have you ever gone to bed one evening without any symptoms but you just knew that you didn't feel exactly right, and awakened in the middle of the night or the next morning with a full-fledged cold? Or have you looked at your child and, while he or she seemed normal on the surface, something inside you said, "I think he or she is getting sick"? I remember one client whose baby was sick, and she called the doctor, who told her to watch the child overnight and bring the baby in the next morning. When my client hung up the phone and went back to her child, before she touched the child she got a strong intuitive sense that she needed to take her baby to the emergency room immediately. By the time mother and child arrived at the hospital, the baby had had a seizure due to a very high fever. If the mother hadn't listened to her intuition and read the child's energy, the baby might have died.

When we access our inner wisdom, we can tap into the body's energy to help ourselves stay healthy. Indeed, both ancient and modern medicine recognize the importance of using the body's energy to help diagnose and heal. Healing systems dating back many thousands of years recognize that health and illness are essentially a function of the free flow of energy throughout the body. While this may sound very alternative, Western-based medicine is finally coming to recognize the body's energetic nature. As Dr. Brownstein reminded me recently, "Conventional medicine utilizes energetic medicine in EKGs, EEGs, nerve conduction studies, MRIs, CAT scans, and PET scans. None of these tests would work if the body wasn't an energetic body. And as doctors take a closer look at the energetic flow of the body, they're going to have to look at an energetic model for health and illness."

Great doctors recognize the importance of tuning in to and working with the body's energy, and they use their own intuitive abilities to do so. (Whether they call it "intuition" or "diagnosis" or "educated guesswork," most doctors use a lot more than just the conscious mind to diagnose and choose treatments for patients.) I'm fortunate to work with some exceptional healers, both conventionally trained doctors and practitioners of alternative medicine. These people take care of me physically and also help me learn more about energy, the body, and how we can use our intuition to read our own health and energy to help prevent illness and stay strong. Dr. Jeffrey Nusbaum, a conventionally trained family physician who expanded his expertise into a wide range of alternative medical techniques, says, "There's an inner wisdom. The body wants to be healed. Disease is not a normal state of the body; it wants to reach equilibrium, to be in a disease-free state. And if you can work with the body's own energy to bring it back into balance, the body will do the rest."

Whether we are experiencing abundant health, suffering from disease, or anything in between, using our inner wisdom with our health is probably one of the most important things we can do. Intuition, our inner knowing, can warn us of health problems before they become serious, so we may address them quickly. Intuition also can help us decide which health professionals and treatments will be best for our needs. Remember, however, that inner wisdom encompasses intuition, logic, and common sense, and you need to use all three in making health decisions. Suppose you are cutting something in the kitchen and inadvertently cut your hand with a kitchen knife. You're bleeding pretty profusely, and you put a compress on the cut. Your intuition may tell you it's nothing serious, but common sense also tells you to get it checked, so you go to the urgent care clinic just in case. Logic should tell you to see a dentist for your teeth and a psychotherapist if you're experiencing emotional issues. But in many cases, your intuition can help you evaluate the diagnoses and prescriptions offered by your medical practitioners. We must tap into our own inner wisdom to help us make the lifestyle and treatment choices that will keep us well or return us to health. Only when we work in partnership with our healers can we use the full power of universal wisdom to help us live the energy-filled, healthy lives we deserve.

Tuning In to Your Health

Tuning in to your health is often a process of getting quiet, asking your body questions, and allowing the responses to come from inside. These responses may come in the form of thoughts, memories, or sensations. Suppose you feel run down or just have a sense that something's not quite right with your health. You can use the intuitive asking steps described in chapter 3 to see what might be causing your discomfort. Your answer may come in the form of a memory of being at work at ten o'clock at night and feeling enormously fatigued. You realize that you worked a lot of hours a couple of weeks ago and you haven't caught up on your sleep yet. Or perhaps something is off with your diet. I have a vegetarian friend who every so often dreams of eating a big steak even though she hasn't had meat in years. She has come to understand that this dream means she needs more protein in her diet. She has fish for dinner the next day, and the dreams stop.

You may recall some emotional event that's still bothering you—an argument you had with your spouse, an upset at work, a problem with your kids, for example. Maybe it's the anniversary of the day you asked your spouse for a divorce, or your child had to go to the hospital, or some other traumatic event. Emotions can upset the delicate balance of many of the systems in the human body, producing digestive problems, skin eruptions, backaches, and so on. You can deny or delay dealing with emotional issues consciously, but their effects may show up physically until you do so.

As we'll discuss later, everything, from what we eat and drink, the lifestyle choices we make, the emotions we experience daily, and our positive and negative thoughts can affect our health, and our intuition can pick up on signals from any of these areas. The most important thing is to be balanced in mind, body, and spirit. People are so involved with their emotional lives that they neglect to use their intuition for their health. And if we don't take care of the body that houses the spirit and the mind, we can find our quality of life diminished and our mind and spirit oppressed.

Medical practitioners, too, will use their intuition to tune in to their patients to diagnose and treat health issues. With the complexities of modern medicine, it's more important than ever that doctors use their intuition to home in on the patient's particular condition. I read recently that there are thousands of diseases, an equal number of conditions caused by deficiencies and excesses in diet and environment, hundreds of drugs and thousands of chemical substances that can produce toxic effects in the body. These thousands of conditions can create around two hundred different symptoms, and many of the symptoms overlap. A headache could mean tension in the neck, the beginning of a migraine, a brain tumor, a stroke, high blood pressure, or a hundred other conditions. One doctor reported that his average patient presented with around forty-nine symptoms at any given time, and symptoms often varied with every visit. While past experience with patients and with different diseases can help doctors diagnose more accurately, there is a point where good doctors tune in to their intuitive sense of what's going on. Medicine isn't just a science; it's also an art. Good doctors use their "gut feelings" along with medical histories and physical exams to guide them to a diagnosis.

Jeffrey Nusbaum once described his own patient workup to me. It includes the same blood work that you find in any conventional medical practice, and a full medical history, with a body chemistry health questionnaire that asks for vague and specific symptoms. Then Jeff reads the questionnaire with the patient present and asks questions along the way. "At the same time I'm getting a sense of the person's constitution," he reports. He told me that in addition to a traditional physical exam, he uses muscle testing, too. (Known as applied kinesiology, muscle testing is one powerful way the body's intuition talks clearly to the care provider.) Dr. Nusbaum and others like him are looking for clues that indicate hormonal, energetic, and/or nutritional imbalances. The goal is to align the body with the spirit, bringing the patient back to wholeness. I'm a huge believer in alternative medicine, whether it is Chinese, ayurvedic, or other modalities.

One of the advantages of alternative medicine is its willingness to ask the body directly for information on what it wants and needs and where the specific weaknesses appear in the system. Jeff Fantich is my chiropractor in Michigan, and while he uses many tests to make a diagnosis, he was trained in applied kinesiology by its founder, Dr. George Goodheart. Applied kinesiology uses muscle testing and other diagnostic means to use the body's own wisdom to diagnose imbalances. Applied kinesiology is like plugging into the body's computer.

The body knows what the problem is, but often the brain doesn't have access to that information. With muscle testing, doctors can access that information and then ask the body for the best treatment to bring the body back into balance. Here's an example: When someone like Dr. Fantich uses muscle testing to speak directly to the body, he might have a patient hold her arm straight out to the side. Dr. Fantich asks the patient to keep her arm up while he applies gentle pressure to push it down. Then Dr. Fantich asks questions about different aspects of the patient's health. He might say the word *liver* while he pushes down, and if the patient is able to keep her arm strong and steady, that means the liver is strong. But if he says "stomach" and all of a sudden the patient's arm can be pushed down easily, that means there is some problem with the stomach. He then follows up with more detailed questions to determine exactly what the problem might be, its origins, and even potential treatment options.

You can try a version of muscle testing yourself. Hold the tips of your thumb and forefinger together, forming a circle. Say, "My name is . . . " and state your name while you use the thumb and forefinger of your other hand to try to break the circle formed by your fingers. Now, say, "My name is John Smith," or some name that is not your own, and try the same thing. Most people find that, while they cannot break the circle formed by their fingers when they say their real name, it's very easy to break the circle when they tell a lie. The body knows the difference between lies and truth. In the same way, it knows when an organ or system is strong or weak. Applied kinesiologists use this wisdom to speak to the body directly and ask about symptoms, causes of illness, and the best treatment for the patient.

My doctor Jeff Fantich had someone come to see him because of pain in the knee. His family doctor had sent him to an orthopedist, and he had had X-rays, an MRI, and exploratory arthroscopic surgery, but they could find no cause for the pain. Using applied kinesiology, Dr. Fantich diagnosed a weakness in the patient's gallbladder. (Every muscle in the body is related to different organs, and there's a small muscle right behind the knee that's related to the gallbladder.) When he treated the gallbladder, the pain in the knee went away.

You may not live in Michigan and see the same doctors I do. That's not the point. The point is that caring alternative providers exist. You may have to do some searching to find them. This is where your intuition and ability to invoke the law of attraction comes into play.

A colleague of mine was having some health problems and she instinctively knew she needed an alternative practitioner. She checked in with her intuition and it confirmed her idea about the sort of person she needed to see. In a quiet space, she invoked the law of attraction and because of the urgency of her situation, she asked that within that day she be sent to exactly the right care provider. In a random phone conversation with a friend about Internet service providers, he mentioned to her that he had started seeing a new doctor just eleven miles from her town! In her gut, she knew instantly that this was the person she had asked for. It turned out to be true.

If you feel your doctor isn't paying attention to your feelings and ideas of what's going on with your health, speak up, and if necessary, change doctors. Your intuition about the doctor being too busy, too tired or overworked, or your logical observation of the same, could be spot on. Your doctor should be your partner in caring for your health, not the boss. He or she may have specialized knowledge, but only you know the inner climate of your own body. Even the most intuitive physicians cannot know the experience of health or illness that is present in your body in any given moment. Ultimately you must be in charge of your own health and well-being.

One of the biggest mistakes we can make is giving away our power when it comes to our health. Doctors are not God: they don't have all the answers. For a lot of us, this is an unnerving idea. Rather than taking responsibility for our own health, we want others to tell us what to do. Hetty Quarrella is a friend and an incredibly talented healer, hypnotherapist, NAET practitioner, and massage therapist. She told me recently, "A lot of people prefer to think of health as something that happens or doesn't. They don't want to take charge because it's too scary." I've heard so many people tell me they are scared of talking to their doctor. They think the doctor will think they are whining hypochondriacs, or pests!

Hetty, like many alternative providers, believes that she and the patient form a team. Your return to wellness has a lot more to do with you than with the practitioners you consult. The doctor's main purpose is to help you help yourself to feel good again.

Illness and Our Inner Wisdom

When energy is abundant and free flowing, we experience health. When this flow is constricted or blocked, we experience disease. Our energy can be decreased by stress, environment, toxins, pathogens, bad habits, even bad thoughts. Unfortunately, many of us have learned to ignore the stress and "dis-stress" signals our body is sending, and thus we find ourselves sick and tired, or worse, seriously ill. We must pay attention to the signals we're given on all fronts, both conscious and intuitive, physical, mental, and emotional, so that we may take care of our health before we develop serious problems.

Illness actually can be a great friend, as it tells us something is wrong before the body stops running altogether. If we didn't get sick, we could keep acting in the same way and exposing ourselves to the same toxins and stresses until they killed us. Have you ever read about leprosy, one of the most feared diseases in the ancient and modern world? Leprosy often afflicted the extremities and could cause numbness in fingers and toes. Lepers could seriously injure a finger on a hot stove, for example, or scrape a toe to the bone without being aware of it. In the same way, without illness to serve as a "red flag" that something is wrong, we would continue hurting ourselves often without knowing it until we did ourselves irreparable harm. In fact, illnesses such as diabetes and high blood pressure are problematic because they often don't present symptoms until they have damaged our internal organs for years.

It's our responsibility to use our intuition to tune in to the signs and signals that our own body gives. Each body has its own unique language; what will cause me to have an upset stomach, for instance, could be exactly what you love to eat. The area of my body that reacts to stress may be very different from your "soft spot." The issue, however, is less what is causing us discomfort and illness and more why this discomfort is arising and what meaning it has for us. Someone once said that any symptom can have a number of causes, and the treatment needed will be determined by the cause. A headache can be caused by bright lights, loud noises, dehydration, muscle tension in the neck or shoulders, a migraine, a brain tumor, toxins in the liver or kidneys—hundreds of different things. You can treat the headache with a pain reliever, but unless you can figure out and treat the cause, the headache will come back, or worse—the problem that caused the headache may indicate a more serious problem that, if left untreated, may harm your health significantly.

That's where intuition and a good diagnosis can help. The conscious mind can tell us what the obvious cause of a headache may be, but your inner wisdom can tap into knowledge that the conscious mind does not have. In conjunction with logic and common sense, your intuition can help guide you to the real source of your illness so you can treat the problem more effectively. You can help your doctor by pointing him or her to whatever cause you sense may be producing your symptoms. And you can use your intuition to feel whether a recommended treatment will be effective or not.

Of course, I'm not saying use only your intuition when it comes to your health. Intuition is only one of the three forces that compose inner wisdom. In the same way that you should eat, exercise, and live to support your health *and* go to your doctor if you need treatment, you need to use logic, common sense, *and* intuition to help you stay as healthy as possible and treat problems while they are minor.

Intuition can be most helpful when dealing with the non-physical forces that can affect our health. The illnesses we experience may have to do with outside forces—including our lifestyle, age, genetics, even socioeconomic class—but they also have to do with the inner forces of our thoughts, feelings, emotions, and perceptions. These inner forces may not even be from this lifetime. My sister Alicia, who does past-life regressions, says that the experiences of past lives have physiological as well as psychological effects. Someone who has a weakness in the lungs may have died by drowning; another who lost a leg in a previous life may have problems in the same leg in this lifetime. While we may not know where our illnesses come from, we can be aware of the presence in our bodies of the early indicators of problems so we can deal with them before they become serious.

When addressing our illnesses or even a diminution of our health, most of us think first of the physical causes. Did we sit next to someone who had a cold? Did we eat or drink something that disagreed with us? Have we been working too hard, or not getting enough sleep? Did we neglect to exercise, or take our vitamins, or go to the dentist, or use sunscreen? Does high blood pressure or diabetes or arthritis run in our family? All of these factors are important to track down and they may very well contribute significantly to our diminished health and well-being. However, when using our inner wisdom to help us avoid illness and gain health, our emotions and our thoughts must be given equal significance.

Anyone who has felt the blush of embarrassment, the warmth of love, the gut-wrenching pain of grief, or the lightness and elation of laughter knows the physiological effects of emotions. Emotions can make us sick or help us get well. They can lengthen our lives or shorten them.

We often tell ourselves we want to manifest optimal health, a fit, trim body, a powerful physique, vibrant energy, and so on. Yet often, by not listening to our intuition, we enslave our bodies in routines, circumstances, and behaviors that are detrimental to us. For instance, a woman who gains an enormous amount of weight to cover up the pain of a bad, loveless marriage, or the person whose hated job is causing such exhaustion after work that exercising is out of the question, are not listening to the subtle intuition from the universe nor to the physical manifestation of their emotions in the outer world.

In their many books on the law of attraction, Esther and Jerry Hicks describe how positive emotions are a sign that you are on the right path and what you are thinking about is good and healthy for you. When you succumb to negative emotions (fear, anger, guilt, envy, etc.) you are attracting more pain into your life, more problems, more of the same. Your intuition is that little voice in your head that monitors your emotions and screams, "Stop! This is hurting us! Don't do this!"

Not expressing your emotions and not having close relationships in which to share our feelings may even make us more susceptible to cancer. Recently I read an article about the effects of stress (an emotion) on our cells. Perceived stress—the way we feel about our situation—can literally shorten the telomeres, the cell markers that determine how many times a cell can replicate. The shorter the telomere, the sooner the cell will die. That's the power of our emotions. Think about it: when someone is upsetting you, you're blocking your energy. You've given him the power over your mood, your health, and your ability to manifest what you want in your life at that moment. The other person is probably walking around oblivious, but there you are, all tied up emotionally. That's hurting your health.

Luckily, we all have the power to change our emotions if they are harming us. Ask yourself, "Is this worth making myself feel sick and miserable over?" Usually, it's not. It's our job to take care of ourselves first, to seize back our power. The way to do this is to change our thoughts. When we change our thoughts, we can change our emotions and thus change our physical bodies. Thoughts are things; they direct our reality. It's been proven time and again that our thoughts can make us sick or well, strengthen or tax our immune systems, even kill us or keep us alive. How we perceive the events of our lives has a direct effect on the emotions we attach to them and how they show up in our bodies. For example, I find that having positive thoughts and putting a protective guard around myself makes for a better night's sleep and a better time when I wake up in the morning. Positive thoughts can give you peace of mind if nothing else, allowing you to start your day with good emotions in your system.

My sister Alicia uses the power of thoughts in the relaxation tapes she makes for her clients. In these tapes, she teaches people to change their negative thoughts. My sister believes that the first step in changing negative thoughts is to become aware we are thinking them. One way to do this is to pay attention for an hour to how many negative thoughts you have. Write them on a sheet of paper (or two or three sheets). Most people cannot believe how many negative things they say about themselves and others in a single hour.

As we know from the timeless law of attraction, every thought we think goes out to the universe, reverberates, and comes back to us magnified. For this reason it is very important to become aware of our thoughts, both negative and positive.

Once you are aware of your negative thoughts, relax. Get into a calm and peaceful space. As my sister suggests, visualize putting the negative thoughts into a helium balloon and letting them fly away, higher and higher, until they disappear. I like to send negative energy back to where it came from. The visualization of negative thoughts leaving is the powerful part, no matter where you imagine they go.

In the vacancy left by the negative thoughts, insert positive thoughts such as *I am okay* or *I can handle this* or *I see myself achieving health now*. Put in as many positive thoughts as you can. If you had twenty items on your list, force yourself to come up with sixty positive ones. Cancel out the negative energy you were allowing in by drowning it in positivity! The more positive thoughts and energy you bring to the situation, the more space there is for healing.

The impact of thoughts and emotions on the body forms the basis of many alternative medical treatments. There is no separation between the body, mind, emotions, and spirit; all are part of the same holistic creation that extends before and after this lifetime and encompasses every thought, emotion, physical sensation, and intuitive impulse we have ever had. For true healing to occur, we must heal ourselves on every level. Changes to the body without changes to our thoughts and emotions will produce some effect, of course; but the effects of changing body, mind, and emotions together will help us attain and maintain our health throughout our lifetime.

Inner Wisdom and Substance Abuse

In my readings, I often pick up chemical imbalances caused by alcoholism, drugs, medications, even certain psychological conditions like depression. When I was in Europe recently, a woman, Patricia, came for a reading. Her husband had killed himself not too long before. Very quickly I tuned in to him and his mother, Rose, who was with him on the other side. "I'm getting the feeling he had mood swings and a chemical imbalance," I said. "The chemistry in his brain was not right. Did he use drugs?" His wife confirmed that he used cocaine.

"When someone goes on drugs they lose control of their lives, and they can be very vulnerable and open to demonic energies playing tricks with them," I told her. "I think he didn't mean to kill himself, but he was on cocaine and saw his mother and fantasized about going to see her. Is there an M in your family? Melissa? Is this your daughter? He wants this to be a good lesson for her and her friends never to use drugs."

I believe that substance abuse is an issue that needs to be addressed not just physically, psychologically, and emotionally, but also intuitively. Many substance abusers both here and on the other side tell me that they started using drugs or alcohol not because it felt good but because they were having problems coping with their lives. Others are just repeating psychological patterns from their past—their parents were dysfunctional or they've been in an abusive relationship.

Some people self-medicate with liquor and drugs because they are extremely sensitive and/or intuitive. They need to learn to protect themselves and their energy so they can live in the world once they get treatment. I also have observed with substance abuse that drugs and alcohol can open people up to malevolent energies. It's almost as if these substances destroy the protective energetic barriers that most people set up for themselves consciously or unconsciously. In the same way drug and alcohol use releases the inhibitions (and feels good for that reason), releasing inhibitions also can leave you open to trickster spirits and other malevolent forces.

Once substance abusers recognize their problems, they

need a lot of support to kick their negative habits. That support comes in the form of physical care for withdrawal, and psychological and emotional care in the form of therapy and twelve-step programs. Twelve-step programs bring four of the most important forces in the universe to an addict's side. First, they force the addict to admit the truth about him- or herself, and in the truth we're freed. Second, they call on a higher power to help the substance abuser. No matter what name you give it, when you appeal to universal goodness and wisdom, it will come to your aid. Third, twelve-step programs call on the substance abuser to exercise willpower. Willpower is a power exercised by our free will—it's a life force that we can use to fight addiction. Fourth, they call on the force of love, both inside and outside. Substance abusers are surrounded by their peers, who offer them love and understanding. This helps addicts develop the self-love that is the only way out of the trap of abuse.

I also believe addicts need care on a higher level to make sure they block negative energies they may have invited in while they were drinking or using. Addiction creates a powerful pull, not just for the addict but also for malevolent forces. They say the devil was a fallen angel, and if someone's been addicted, it's possible that negative energy knows their "address," so to speak. I counsel people whose loved ones are coming off an addiction to surround the person with a white light of protection at all times. I teach them my prayer of protection and if the former addict is open to it, I ask him or her to say it regularly. I also ask them to use their inner wisdom when a craving comes up, to point them toward what the real problem is that they're trying to avoid with drugs or alcohol. While logic and common sense can tell someone to call a sponsor or to go get something to eat, listening to our inner voice often is the only way we can get to the heart of what has produced the behavior and change it at its root. If nothing else, turning to inner wisdom instead of a "fix" can help an addict to open up to the good side of universal energy, to goodness, gratitude, love, and other positive emotions. Then the addict can choose to turn away from the other ways of feeling good and toward energy that will be better for him or her in the long run.

We are built to resonate with the highest levels of energy. Like a tuning fork, when that energy shows up we feel the same "note" inside ourselves and start vibrating at a higher level. We must focus on coming into resonance with the highest, using our willpower, self-love, prayer, meditation—anything that works for us. Above all, we must tell the truth about and to ourselves. Addictions cannot stand up to truth because truth is the foundation of universal wisdom. Only when we tell the truth can we walk the path away from addiction and toward health and wholeness.

Food, Water, and Energy

In the same way we use our logic, common sense, and intuition to keep ourselves healthy, we must use all three when it comes to the food choices we make. Other than air, there is nothing that determines our daily sense of well-being more than what we eat and drink. Every substance we take into or apply to our bodies will affect our health and well-being. That's why diet and proper hydration are such important elements of our health. Often, however, we forget the energetic side of food and water. Every food has energy, and water is one of the primary conduits of energy in the body. If the foods we eat aren't providing us with the nutrients we need, our cells can't produce energy and our vitality can plummet. If we don't get enough water—and far too many of us don't—then our cells shrivel, stick together, and cease to allow energy to flow throughout the body. We can use our inner wisdom to sense the effects of the foods we eat and the amount of water we drink, and to help us make the best choices possible for optimum health.

After testing many patients with blood work and urine, hair, and muscle testing, Dr. David Brownstein has found that most of us are mineral, salt, and vitamin deficient. Chronic illnesses like arthritis, cancer, or autoimmune disorders can be caused or exacerbated by nutritional deficiencies. "The body is a wonderful thing; it should be able to take care of itself given the proper materials," he says. "But many times people are missing the basic building blocks of what they need, and the body starts shutting down to preserve itself. You've got to figure out the underlying cause of the symptoms from a nutritional standpoint and treat that." (Dr. Brownstein has written a lot of great books on nutrition, natural hormones, and how to care for yourself holistically. You can check his website, www.drbrownstein.com, for more information.)

In the same way we ignore the body's intuitive signals of disease, we've also learned to ignore what foods we truly need and how much water we need to drink. In America, we've become a nation of obese food addicts, craving our fixes of high-fat, high-sugar fast foods washed down with gallons of soda pop. We no longer recognize the subtle signals of satiation as we continue to stuff ourselves to the point of nausea. To top off our dysfunctional food habits, what we eat is processed, which eliminates any real nutrition, and filled with preservatives, additives, and pesticides. It's no wonder we continue to eat past the point of satiation—our food no longer has any nutrition left to satisfy the body's true needs!

Of course, many of us eat to satisfy needs that have nothing to do with nutrition and the creation of energy. Food has an emotional component, too. Just like alcohol or drugs, food can be a narcotic, deadening us to emotions we don't want to face. Because food can affect our energy, in some circumstances it also can keep us from accessing our intuitive force. I have to be very careful of what I eat when I'm doing several readings in a row, because certain foods can affect my stamina and ability to be the clearest channel possible. I can still give readings, but it's a lot more difficult to keep focused and clear when I'm not eating well.

To gain the most from the food we eat, we need to use our inner wisdom in three ways. First, we need to use common sense in our choices of the foods we consume. We need to recognize that food is primarily supposed to provide us with energy. Preservatives, processed foods, and food loaded with fats and sugars do not give us energy other than in the moment, and they clog our systems rather than letting the energy flow freely. To increase energy, we should eat organic produce and meats, whole grains, and foods that have been minimally processed.

Second, we need to choose food based on what the body truly craves. Our body knows what it needs but our thoughts and emotions can get in the way of listening to it. Before you eat, use your intuition to check in and see what you really want. If you feel a craving for something you know is bad for you, check to see if you're using food to suppress an emotional need or worrisome thought and figure out a different way to handle your emotions. Your inner wisdom will help guide you to understanding the difference between physical and emotional needs, and lead you to fill yourself up appropriately.

Third, we need to listen for the signals that we are satisfied. One of the best ways to learn when you are full is to eat consciously. Make eating the only activity you are undertaking at mealtime. The Buddhists practice "mindfulness," in which they pay attention to every moment and every action, including eating. Mindful eating allows you to hear the inner voices of enjoyment and of satiation more clearly. Again, intuition can help you sense fullness even before your stomach signals your conscious mind.

We're finding out more and more about the importance of water to our health. Our bodies are 70 percent water, and nothing happens inside us without its presence. I find it very interesting that whenever I get an alternative medicine treatment or massage, the practitioner suggests I drink water afterward. Water flushes out toxins and keeps everything, including our energy, flowing. Now with the work of Masaru Emoto we are coming to understand the ability of water to carry not just nutrients but also information within us. Emoto is doing research on imprinting water with vibrational energy and using it to heal people of different diseases and conditions. While this research is still in its infancy, to me it makes sense that this substance that is present in all of our cells and makes life possible would be used by universal wisdom as a conduit of information and healing. Emoto suggests that we "charge" water before we drink it by praying over it and putting our positive intention into the water. I grew up saying grace before meals, asking God to bless the food to our use—perhaps it's the same thing. I believe that putting positive thoughts and energy into every substance we put into our bodies can only help us use those substances to our benefit.

If you want an example of the power of such substances as food and water to affect one's energy, think of allergies. In some cases even the smallest amount of a substance that is harmless to most people—such as peanuts—can cause some-one to keel over and die. Conventional medicine treats al-lergies with drugs to suppress the symptoms and counteract the allergic reaction, but alternative medicine often takes a different approach. My friend Hetty is certified in NAET, a new way to treat allergies. NAET stands for Nambudripad's Allergy Elimination Techniques, Dr. Devi S. Nambudripad being the originator of these particular therapies. NAET rec-ognizes that there is a physical and emotional component to most allergic responses. The practitioner uses neuromuscular sensitivity testing (NST) to compare the strength and weak-ness of any muscle of the body in the presence and absence of a substance. If there is no allergy, the muscle will test strong; the presence of weakness signals a problem. When the body responds that it is allergic to a substance, the practitioner uses a variety of treatments, including acupressure, homeopathy, and nutrition to reprogram the body to no longer react in the same way. After as little as one treatment, the patient can be in the presence of the allergen without a problem.

NAET shows us once again the intertwined nature of the mind, emotions, and body. The way we become allergic to a substance often has to do with a past incidence of linking emo-tions to it. In the same way we can have a bad experience with a dog, for example, and afterward become phobic of dogs, we can become allergic to a food, a substance, or even a person if the emotion we felt around them was strong enough. Hetty tells a story of a client who kept talking about meat. Now, one of the strange things about allergies is that we often crave what we're allergic to. (Our body needs the nutrients in that particular food, but because the body is allergic it can't process the food when it receives it. It still needs the nutrients, though, so it keeps asking for the food.) Hetty thought she'd check her client for meat allergies. Sure enough, she tested positive, so Hetty treated her using NAET. After twenty minutes, Hetty came back into the treatment room and the client said, "I remember where this came from." When she was a teenager she had gone out with friends for hamburgers, and as she was eating, her boyfriend walked into the restaurant with another girl. The linkage of the feelings with the meat had created the allergic reaction. By eliminating the physical reaction, NAET can help clear the emotion and restore the free flow of energy in the body.

Our bodies are remarkable assemblages of energy and when we provide them with the right mix of food, water, nutrients, supplements, and nutritional support, they will be fit and happy vessels for our minds and spirits. As Dr. Brownstein says, "The body knows what to do; it just needs the right formula."

Using Universal Energy to Heal

When we are experiencing disease, we can use our intuition to tap into the body's wisdom and its innate ability to heal. Healing is never just a matter of drugs, surgery, or even alternative medical treatments such as herbs, massage, acupuncture, and so on. Healing only occurs when the body accepts such treatments and uses the energy they provide to restore its own energetic and physical balance. As every doctor or health practitioner will tell you, the same treatment given to different patients with the same symptoms and conditions can produce vastly different results. Using the power of our inner wisdom and our intention to heal, we can tap into the body's true needs and encourage it to accept the treatments provided to bring back health.

More and more scientific studies are demonstrating the power of energy and intention when it comes to healing. For instance, in one study healers were asked to send energy to red blood cells that had been put into test tubes of distilled water. (Distilled water kills red blood cells, which require a pH close to that of blood plasma.) Working from another room and using the power of intention and their innate intuitive abilities to send energy to blood cells in one group of test tubes, the healers were able to significantly slow the damage to the test blood cells, compared to a control group. In another study, healers sent energy remotely to patients with high blood pressure. Neither the doctors nor the patients knew who was receiving the healing energy and who was not until after the experiment was completed. Statistical analysis showed that those patients who received healing energy experienced a significant improvement in systolic blood pressure compared to the other subjects in the test.

I think part of the desire to learn more about energetic healing comes from a growing disillusionment with what modern medicine has to offer. Don't get me wrong: modern medicine is fantastic. Its diagnostic abilities are wonderful; its ability to treat trauma and acute illness is unsurpassed. If I or someone I loved was suffering a heart attack or stroke or was in an accident, you'd better believe we'd get to the hospital immediately. But there are healing forces in the universe that go far beyond the drugs and surgery of conventional medicine, and I believe those healing forces can be extremely valuable in restoring us to full health. We tap into those healing energies through our intention and our intuition.

A few years ago I saw this interplay in my own family. My sister Alicia's niece was in the sixth month of her second pregnancy, and she was having a terrible time. She couldn't keep anything down and had had to go to the hospital several times to be rehydrated. However, this time she got sicker after the rehydration. They did an X-ray and found a shadow on her heart—a tumor the size of a golf ball. She was taken by helicopter to the university hospital in Ann Arbor, Michigan, where they performed emergency surgery. She was on a respirator and a heart-lung machine, and when she came out of surgery there were several complications. The baby died and they had to put her through labor; and then she had a seizure and her head swelled up. The doctors were not optimistic. "The only hope you have is a miracle," one of them said. "It's in God's hands; we can't do anything more for her."

"Good!" Alicia said. "It's in good hands, then." Alicia and I believe in the power of prayer and positive thoughts, and we know how powerful intention and energetic healing can be. So she called me in California to ask me what my reading was on the situation. I used my psychic gift to tune in to her niece, and told Alicia exactly where she needed to focus healing energy to bring this young woman back to health. Alicia called Sandy, a dear friend of our family who is a very gifted energy healer, and she did long-distance energy healing to re-build the niece's brain, heart, and nervous system. Our entire family was up day and night for weeks. And then this young woman woke up! They put her on the heart transplant list and put a heart pump in her chest, but Alicia spoke from her own intuitive sense, saying, "She's not going to need a transplant—we're going to get her heart working again." A few weeks later they took out the heart pump and the niece came home. Her recovery was a tribute to her dedicated doctors, all the energy healers who worked on her, and the positive thoughts and prayers she received from so many people.

Some of the problems with modern medicine arise when we ask it to treat chronic conditions for which there is no cure. Diabetes, high blood pressure, arthritis, some cancers, nerve diseases like Parkinson's, autoimmune diseases—for many of these the therapies offered are designed to manage symptoms rather than to cure the problem. Managing symptoms can be helpful, but wouldn't it be better to address the causes of these conditions and perhaps use the body's own wisdom to help return it to balance and health?

That's what much of alternative medicine seeks to accomplish. It's no accident that over two-thirds of the U.S. population has tried at least one kind of alternative treatment in their lives. Most people are looking for ways to restore themselves to health that (1) don't involve drugs with their many side effects and (2) can treat subacute conditions that cause us discomfort and inconvenience but aren't perhaps bad enough to put us in the hospital. More important, we're looking to tap into the innate intuitive intelligence of our bodies to tell us what we need to become healthy again. As David Brown-stein says, "Long-term use of drugs that treat symptoms is not good." We all must recognize our need to use natural things that actually build the body up and help with healing. Most conditions can be treated naturally. You simply need to search for the underlying causes of disease and use natural means to build the body up.

The body knows what it wants, and it is always looking for the right energetic fit when it comes to the healing it needs. There are hundreds of healing modalities that you can use, in addition to your own inner wisdom, to diagnose where your body is deficient, and restore balance and bring energy back to the body, resulting in greater health. I consult with all kinds of health practitioners depending on the conditions I'm experiencing. I go to an OB/GYN, a dentist, a chiropractor, a massage therapist, an energy worker, and a nutritionist. I try to choose doctors who embrace alternative medicine along with conventional approaches because I believe they are more in tune with the power of intuition and energy to heal and maintain the body.

One of the energetic healing techniques that I've had personal experience with is the SCIO machine. Both Dr. Nusbaum in Michigan and my chiropractor in Los Angeles, Dr. Robert Vinson, use the SCIO. It's a sophisticated computer-based system that was developed by Dr. William Nelson, who was a mathematician and physicist in the U.S. space program. The SCIO scans the electrical energy of the body, using 110 channels to evaluate over 12,000 frequencies at a speed of approximately $1/100$ of a second for each. It measures the resonances and reaction in your body and compares the readings to stored records of optimum readings. Like a virus scan for your computer, the SCIO can detect nutritional deficiencies, diseases, food sensitivities, allergies, and viruses.

It shows you where your system is weak energetically. I've been on the SCIO machine several times, and it's brought up physical problems before I had any noticeable symptoms and confirmed results that I received from a blood test. In a way, the SCIO is kind of an electrical version of intuition in that it spots problems before they ever really surface. But the SCIO is not just a diagnostic tool. Once it scans the body's electrical energy and pinpoints anomalies and weaknesses, it uses any of seventy energetic therapies to harmonize the body's stresses and imbalances and return the body to health by counteracting the stressors that caused disease in the first place. After I was hooked up to the SCIO and sat for a few minutes, the sinus infection that I was developing got much better.

Alternative medicine techniques—including NAET, acupuncture, chiropractic, homeopathy, herbal medicine, nutritional healing, chakra balancing, massage, cleansing, and many other bioenergetic balancing practices—are designed to help increase your body's level of health. Some of them are systemic treatments that bring more energy into the body as a whole; others are focused on treating one particular problem or issue. But alternative medicine treatments as a whole share two characteristics. First, they are designed to work with the body's energy rather than imposing change from the outside. Second, their goal is to bring the body back into balance. The belief is that the body has its own intelligence and, if given the right support, it will function at the highest possible level. Dr. Brownstein puts it like this: "If you think of your health as a pie composed of many pieces, you can either treat the entire pie or treat individual pieces. Sometimes you can't do much for the whole pie, but if you can improve enough pieces of it, the whole body will get better."

Your Wisest Approach to Health

While I'm obviously a huge fan of energetic healing, I'm not saying do only this. In the same way that inner wisdom encompasses logic, common sense, and intuition, I believe that caring for your health should encompass conventional as well as alternative medicine. I go for mammograms and pap smears; I have annual checkups and visit a number of doctors to evaluate my health. I also go to chiropractors, I use natural hormones to keep my system in balance, I get massages and energy balancing, and I take vitamins, herbs, and other supplements. I'm interested in benefiting from the best that both conventional and alternative medicine have to offer, so I can stay healthy for a long, long time.

You also should not expect miracles from one session with an alternative healer. I once read, for example, that when you go to conventional doctors, they don't give you just one pill. Instead, they ask you to take medication over a period of time. In the same way, you probably will need more than one treatment from a healer to bring your body back to balance and health. Your health didn't get the way it is in only one day, so you shouldn't expect your healing to happen that quickly either. And always, always consult your inner wisdom when it comes to any treatment or health practitioner. Just as there are good and bad lawyers, teachers, psychologists, and intuitives, there are good and bad doctors. You want to surround yourself with those who are ethical and whose intentions are pure.

One of the greatest gifts and greatest perils in the modern age is the variety of treatments that are offered. We must call on all our inner resources as well as external support to choose what is right for us. There are ways to diagnose and support our health energetically, and there are ways to diagnose and support it medically. You have to be really attuned to yourself to determine what you need. Use your inner wisdom—logic, common sense, and intuition—to monitor your health and choose the appropriate care based on what you sense. As Dr. Jerome Groopman, a professor at Harvard Medical School, wrote, "Evaluating medical advice is the greatest challenge for every patient. Armed with knowledge, steadied by family and friends, and calling on intuition, we can gain clarity and insight, and are prepared to make the best possible decisions."

Finally, remember that in seeking health you must restore your body, mind, and spirit, for they are all part of the same thing. You cannot treat one without affecting the other. The ancient Greeks and Romans sought to have "a sane mind in a sound body." I would add to that equation a happy and balanced spirit that is connected through love to others as well as the divine. When body, mind, and spirit are balanced and filled with energy, then we will have the blooming, abundant health we deserve.

6

Finding and Cherishing
Intuitive Love

One word
Frees us from all the weight and pain of life:
That word is love.

—Sophocles

Being in a great relationship is like no other feeling on earth. It's as if you have a partner, a "better half," someone who is in your corner no matter what. It often seems you're intuitively linked with him; your partner will start to say something and you'll find it's exactly what you were just thinking, or he'll call just as you were picking up the phone to call him. Conversely, a bad relationship feels like hell on earth. There's no communication; your intuition is warning you that you're growing apart. Your energies are not in sync. You feel blocked and stymied in the part of life that once caused so much joy. If life is a school and we're here to learn, relationships are the "advanced studies" classes. Relationships are magnifiers: they show us what's great about ourselves and where we are not so great. They give us more and demand more of us than any other aspect of our lives. To paraphrase poet Emily Dickinson, they are all we know of heaven, and all we need of hell.

We relate because we were made to. We were born to connect with and love others. Relationships remind us of our own true nature and connect us to the universal love that composes everything and everyone. In relationships, love and intuition work hand in hand, one strengthening the other. The love we feel for our partners, our families, our friends, even our pets can increase and deepen our intuitive rapport with them. And our intuition can help us communicate with those we care about across the miles and years, even across the barrier of life and death. Here on earth, we can tap into that same energy to attract compatible partners, avoid those who aren't right for us, deepen our relationships with the people in our lives, or perhaps fulfill a karmic destiny with someone romantically or emotionally. We can fine-tune our intuition to be able to read the signals of attraction and/or danger coming our way; we can learn to pick up on and interpret the energy our loved ones are putting out so we can respond to their needs. We also can use intuition to sense present or future problems, tuning in to unspoken causes of trouble. Finally, we can recognize when our intuition is telling us if it's time to leave a relationship and move on.

Is This the One for Me?

If we had to choose partners solely based on logic and common sense, the only way we'd find someone to date is with the kind of questionnaires people fill out when they use a dating service. Happily, most of us tend to add instincts and intuition to the mix to help us decide whether a person is right for us. Some of us are fortunate enough to have the gift of love at first sight. For the rest of us, finding Mr. or Ms. Right begins with a search for Mr. or Ms. Maybe, and a large part of that search begins with sensing energy. We can walk down the street and easily sense the energy of the people we meet. Often we can tell immediately when we encounter someone who has "potential," as one of my girlfriends says. At other times that sense of potential develops once we've gotten to know the other person and we feel the possibility of a connection that lies beneath the surface.

The law of attraction teaches us that we attract what we think about—whether it's good or bad. If we're walking down that same street, thinking about a former lover who hurt us terribly, we are broadcasting to the intuition of everyone we pass that "I'm not emotionally available to love someone new because I'm busy being angry about the past." When we walk down the street feeling good, positive, and strong about ourselves, we broadcast to the intuition of everyone we pass that we are available, open, and desirable. You can practice this. Stand in the produce section of a store and silently transmit loving energy and positive wishes to any other person you see in that area. Wait a few moments. Normally, the other person's intuition will pick it up subconsciously and he'll lift his head and smile—or at least glance at you.

While we may not be able to articulate it, we all know when someone's energy is attractive to us—unless past circumstances get in the way of our intuition. Many people can develop energy blocks around relationships. These blocks are often self-inflicted; they can be caused by dysfunctional habits born of past relationships with parents, siblings, or lovers, or even relationships from previous lifetimes. In one pattern I see with many clients, people didn't get approval or attention from one of their parents. In trying to heal that lack, they are then attracted to partners who have the same energy as the parent that neglected them, and the dysfunctional relationship plays itself out again and again. Wherever they originate, energy blocks can keep you from noticing potential relationships even when they're staring you in the face.

Sometimes our present circumstances can keep us closed to relationships as well. Maybe you're coming off a bad marriage and need time to heal. Maybe you're focused completely on taking care of kids or parents, or you're working eighty hours a week on your career. While you may say, "I want a relationship, but I can't seem to meet anyone," the universe isn't going to put someone in your path just for you to turn him down because you're too busy! To attract a potential partner using your intuition, you must be ready for that relationship to enter your life. That means handling any past or present barriers, and getting rid of any residue from old, painful relationships. Have you ever known someone who has gotten out of a bad relationship only to get right back into the exact same dysfunctional situation again? If you didn't learn your lesson the first time you will probably be doomed to repeat the same bad relationship "class" until you do. Make things easier on yourself: when you leave a bad relationship, do your best to figure out the lesson so you can "graduate" to a better partner the next time around. Some kind of psychological counseling might be good as well. I'm a great advocate of therapy; it helps us clear our minds and emotions so our intuition can flow clearly and we can be happier. I often suggest clients get therapeutic help if I sense any energy blocks caused by their dysfunctional relationship patterns.

Luckily, many of the people we attract into our lives are brought there for our higher good, and that includes those to whom we are attracted romantically. Mr. or Ms. Right is out there; in fact, I believe there can be many Mr. and Ms. Rights for each of us, depending on our circumstances, our stage of life, and the lessons we are meant to learn. The best way we can prepare for our own Mr. or Ms. Right is to be happy just as we are. The worst thing we can do is to put out an energy of desperation or need. Some people just cannot be alone and feel they have to be in a relationship. But to find a healthy relationship you have to get your life in order and be content with yourself first. To attract love you must begin with self-love. You need to acknowledge your own completeness before you will attract the same energy into your life when it's time. When you are genuinely open to a new relationship—when you clear your emotional blockages, stop making excuses, and move "relationship" higher up your priority list—you'll be surprised how many more eligible partners will show up. And once your energy is clear, you can use your intuition to tune in to what others are sending you, so you can evaluate potential partners and avoid those who are less likely to work out. Many of my clients ask me to tell them about their relationships. "Is this the man or woman for me?" they ask. I usually reply, "What do *you* feel? What's your intuitive hit about this person?" People can be far more intuitive for themselves than I am, if they take the time to tune in.

When falling in love, you need to know the other person's true intent; you must see him clearly and he must see you clearly as well. Remember, after a while looks become unimportant, but the soul and spirit of your partner will continue to shape your life. Pay attention to your first hit when you meet someone in the course of your daily life. Check your responses to the people who are already in your environment, as it's possible that a potential partner has been around you for a while but you either weren't aware or weren't ready for the relationship to blossom.

The most frequent relationship questions I get asked are about soul mates. "Will I ever meet my soul mate?" "What if my soul mate shows up and I don't recognize him or her?" Soul mates are not necessarily born as our romantic partners every time. You could have a soul mate who is your child, brother or sister, parent, or best friend. A soul mate can be anyone who helps your soul to grow. As author and medical intuitive Caroline Myss teaches, soul mates can make you happy and they can make you crazy. Soul mates are here to help us learn lessons, and those lessons can be pleasant or otherwise.

Soul mates do exist; there are relationships that are so strong that they last beyond one lifetime and past the grave. Last year I gave a reading for the families of a teenage couple who had been killed in an automobile accident. I told the families that while these young people were very sad for those they had left behind, they were very happy to be together. "They're saying that if one had died and the other didn't, they would have been miserable, because they were true soul mates—they would have stayed together forever," I said. "They don't want you to waste your sadness on them, because they're happy."

I've encountered many relationships that seemed to be predestined. One of my agents was in her late thirties; she'd been in a relationship for ten years and never wanted to get married. But on her first date with a new man, they went out on his boat in the canals of Amsterdam. They stopped to get gas and to walk her dog. As she was walking along the side of the canal, she looked back at him as he worked with the boat and thought, *So that's what my husband looks like.* It surprised her completely, but shortly afterward they became engaged.

When I read for her a few months before her wedding, the spirit of her grandmother Laura kept showing me red roses. "What's that about?" I asked. She told me that her fiancé had been giving her one red rose every week, and as part of their wedding she planned to ask him, "Will you marry me?" and then hand him a red rose. She said that her grandmother had told her never to get married, and so she felt the red rose symbolized her grandmother's blessing.

Sometimes we get into relationships with people because we have a karmic link with them from a past life. You could have been a mother who abandoned her child, and in your next lifetime your child comes back as the lover who dumps you. Or perhaps you were in a Romeo and Juliet situation where your lover died before you could have the relationship you wanted. In your next life you find each other and live together as a happy couple for fifty-plus years. Or you met someone whom you didn't like at first, but eventually he or she became your best friend or a romantic partner. In such cases, I believe that perhaps you and that person shared a past life in which something happened, and the person has come back into your life to heal the relationship. No matter whether it's a result of karma or past lives or soul mates, there can be more than one Mr. or Ms. Right out there for each of us, because our souls need different things to grow at different times. Our responsibility is to tune in to our partners intuitively when they come into our lives to make sure they are right for us, and continue to use our inner wisdom as the relationship develops.

Of course, sometimes we can misinterpret what our intuition is telling us about another person. I read for someone who told me that she was dating a guy named Mike, and she felt strongly that she was going to end up with him. Well, he wasn't ready for a relationship, so they broke up. She wound up marrying the next man she dated—who also was named Mike! Her intuition had been right about the name but wrong about the guy, and definitely wrong about the timing. But when the next Mike appeared, this woman used her intuition to decide if this was the long-term commitment she had been waiting for. Her inner "yes" was strong—and was backed up by the second Mike's proposal.

Sometimes what we think of as the right partner is just wishful thinking. We fall in love with a fantasy—our ideal picture of who we think this person is rather than who he really is. We get attracted by a quality or something we share, or perhaps we're just attracted by the energy someone puts out, and we ignore other character or personality flaws. We're like a horse with blinders on—we see only the road in front of us and miss other important landmarks. (You must have heard the saying "Love is blind.") But riding the road of relationships with blinders is not only foolish, it's dangerous. How many women and men have ended up in abusive relationships because they just didn't allow themselves to pick up on the warning signs early? How many divorced friends have told you, "He just wasn't the person I thought he was"? To find a long-term relationship, we have to take the blinders off and use all our inner wisdom at every step along the way.

Remember, love comes in many forms and is expressed in many ways, and romance is only one form. There are many partners out there for all of us. Your next (or current) partner may or may not be your soul mate, but he or she serves some universal purpose in your life. When I read for a client once, I picked up on a relationship she had recently entered into. "This relationship feels like it has a lot of potential if you both work on it," I told her. "The best relationships are the ones that grow over time as we get to know the other person. Not everything is predestined; we create a lot of our own destiny, especially when it comes to relationships." Whether someone is your soul mate or not, what happens in a relationship is a direct result of the choices you both make.

When you reach the point where you feel ready to commit to a long-term relationship, it's really important to bring intuition, logic, and common sense into the picture. However, often these three forces can seem to be at war. Our hearts tell us one thing when our heads say another, and it's hard to know what should have the greatest weight. Sometimes people choose a romantic partner based only on chemistry. Then, when they get to know the person, they have nothing in common. And in Western cultures the idea of choosing a partner based on logic or what looks good on paper alone seems rather cold. The best relationships are those where there's been a long friendship, where you truly get to know each other. I suggest that you use the three pillars of inner wisdom to go beyond attraction and see the person with whom you want to share your life. It's not about denying attraction or denying common sense; it's about honoring *all* the sources of wisdom that are available to you.

Let me give you a few examples of intuition, logic, and

common sense in relationships. We all have people with whom we spend a lot of time due to work, social activities, and so on. These are the people with whom it would make sense to develop a relationship. Or perhaps your friends and family are trying to fix you up with someone. In these cases, you can rely on your intuition to tell you whether there's even the possibility of a relationship with any of these candidates. Suppose you're attracted to someone who's twenty years younger. If you wish to make this something long term you'd better evaluate the relationship based on logic (for example, odds are that you will probably die before your partner will, so you need to make plans accordingly). Or maybe your new love is secretive about her finances or her past: common sense tells you to find out more about her before you commit to a lasting relationship.

Relationships are fundamentally about the energy created between two people, and the fun starts when you explore the energy dynamic between you. Relationships are also our most accurate mirror, reflecting what we like about ourselves and our partners, what we dislike, and what drives us crazy. We attract what we are, not what we want. What pushes your buttons in your partner may be something you don't like in yourself. What you love in your partner may be a quality you sense in yourself and value.

Check in constantly with your inner wisdom. Here are a few questions you can ask:

- How does this relationship make you feel? Of course, there are going to be ups and downs, but overall do you feel energized and uplifted by this relationship, or do you feel drained?

- How are you together? Do you feel like you are really similar in outlook, taste, energy, or is your partner a great complement to you, bringing qualities to the relationship that you lack?

- When you think of spending the rest of your life with this person, what's your first hit? Remember, our connections with people can be a result of past life ties, and you could be misinterpreting the kind of relationship you have with this person. He or she could be meant to be your best friend, or may have been your lover or child in a previous lifetime and you're feeling the karmic connection.

You need to know yourself well first so you can understand what's going on in the relationship, so use your inner wisdom. Choose based on your intuition, logic, and common sense; be willing to look at your potential partners (and yourself) with honesty when it comes to the traits and qualities you want in a relationship; and then go for it—create your destiny the way you want it to be.

Your Family, Chosen or Otherwise

Some of our most important relationships aren't romantic, but are those with our friends and family. And in the same way our romantic partners provide us with life lessons, so do our family and friends. I believe that before we come into this life we choose our parents and to be born into a particular family because there are relationships from past lives that must be played out and lessons to be learned with these people.

Every relationship is dynamic and we must recognize and acknowledge the changes as our children grow and our parents age. As children, we learn how to relate from our parents and other adults we see around us. When we grow up, we apply those lessons in our other relationships. The problem arises, however, when those lessons are not good ones. I think there's been a lot of dysfunctional parenting in our world, and this can cause difficulties when children grow up. People are looking for the love they failed to get from their mothers and fathers, and they continue the dysfunctional patterns they learned at home.

Recently I read for a young couple, and I quickly picked up that the young man had problems with his father, Carl, who had never approved of the son and was very harsh with him. There was an energy block in the young couple's relationship that came from the father-son dynamic. "Just because he's your dad doesn't mean he's right," I said. "You're allowing your father's negativity to affect this relationship, and that's a mistake. Your fiancée's parents love you, and they'll help you both create a stable, loving family environment. But don't continue giving your dad power over your relationship. He's just not worth it." Both the son and his fiancée were grateful for this advice and left promising they would create a new loving family together.

As a psychotherapist who does a lot of family counseling, my sister Alicia can attest to the influence of our parents when it comes to our ability to relate to others. She agrees that it's critical to be clear about the patterns we pick up from our parents; this is part of knowing ourselves and also preparing ourselves to build healthy relationships as adults. We can use our common sense, logic, and intuition to examine the ways we relate to others and determine if these are ineffective patterns we learned as children. Here are a few questions to help you determine some of your patterns:

- Are you a "people pleaser"?

- Are you bossy or withdrawn or demanding or cold?

- Do you have problems letting others get close to you?

- Do you tend to submerge yourself in a relationship and lose any sense of who you are as a separate person?

- Do any of your partner's traits remind you of parents, stepparents, grandparents, aunts, uncles, or any other adult who might have had an influence on you when you were a child?

- More important, are you ready to get rid of these patterns and develop new ones that will make you happier in your relationships today?

Sometimes merely identifying where a pattern comes from will enable us to let go of it. At other times we may need professional help to move ahead. But our responsibility as adults is to take the best from our parents and leave the rest behind.

Our relationships with sisters and brothers also create a lifelong dynamic that can teach us much about love. Someone once said that parents will pass and friends and lovers come and go, but siblings are part of your life from birth to death. We are both students and teachers of our siblings; they are our closest contemporaries in childhood and throughout our lives. But it's no accident that one of the earliest stories in the Bible is about sibling rivalry: Cain and Abel. Our strong connection with siblings can engender strong ties and create deep wounds. We need to find the balance between loving our siblings and seeing them for who they are, including their strengths and weaknesses.

I was very lucky in my relationships with my two sisters, Alicia and Elaine; we've always been extremely close. We often find ourselves intuitively attuned, calling each other at the same time, having the same hit about a person or situation, and so on. Alicia and I often work together helping people with their issues. Many brothers and sisters tell me they feel strong bonds with their siblings. Unfortunately, these same strong bonds also can create a lot of pain. One woman who called in when I appeared on *Larry King Live* started to cry when I mentioned her sister Barbara. Barbara had always been jealous of her sister and had pushed this woman away from her family. I suggested this woman get counseling and stop giving her sister power over her. Sometimes, even when you wish otherwise, you just have to let a relationship go because it's too toxic. Our sisters and brothers have been part of our lives, but how much they continue to be is up to us.

Friends are the family we choose: they can be soul mates, the result of karma from past lives, even angels for us here on earth. Friends can help us grow and become more or encourage us in our bad habits and behaviors. That's why it's important to choose your friends wisely and use your inner wisdom to evaluate the friendships you have. Do your friends have your best interests at heart? When you're with them, do you feel uplifted or dragged down? Have your friends grown with you, and vice versa? Just like every relationship in your life, your friendships should uplift you, support you, give you love, and help you learn life lessons. Make sure you have the right friends in your life, and that you are the right kind of friend for others.

I couldn't talk about relationships without mentioning pets. For many of us, our relationships with our pets are some of the dearest we have. To the world you may be one person, but to your pet, you may mean the world. Many times in my readings deceased pets will come through, to the delight of their former owners. Our pets also can signal us when our deceased loved ones are nearby. I read for a young woman, Anne, whose pilot fiancé, Donald, had been killed in an airplane crash. Donald came through and told her that he would always love her and be near. Then he showed me a pet of some kind. I asked Anne if she had a dog or cat, and she said she had gotten a dog after Donald had died. "Do you ever see the dog looking over and barking at something, only nobody's there?" I asked. "Yes," she answered. "I told the dog to let me know if Donald is here." The love of pets is unconditional and uncomplicated. Whether on this side or in the other world, our pets can teach us very profound lessons about how to give and care and receive and just plain be.

Loving—and Sometimes Leaving

Once you're in a committed relationship, things get easy, right? Wrong—as anyone who's ever been in one knows, the daily work to keep a relationship living and growing is tough. Relationships go through stages; they're great at times and then they get hard. We love the person and sometimes we don't like him or her, but then we communicate and we fall even deeper in love. Every relationship takes time, work, understanding, and patience. Over the course of any relationship you're guaranteed to hate your partner, be bored with your partner, not want to be around your partner, not be attracted to your partner, be angry/frustrated/upset with your partner, perhaps all in the same week! To top it off, sometimes it seems that your partner expects you not only to use your intuition but to be a mind reader as well. I give anyone great kudos for making a relationship work, because it's not easy.

If emotions like love, respect, honesty, gratitude, and compassion are the foundation of a great relationship, empathy, intuition, and good communication will keep the relationship strong. In relationships many emotions are implied rather than stated. We don't tell our partners all day, every day how we feel about them; we expect them to infer our emotions from our actions. And we also rely on our partner's empathy and intuition to sense our emotions so we don't have to express them out loud. We "know" our partner loves us, we say, whether or not he tells us or shows us every day. We expect this ongoing intuitive, unspoken connection to be part of our intimate relationships.

Sometimes we get insecure and expect our partners to be mind readers; we want them to say "I love you" without our having to ask. But that's not realistic or helpful when it comes to building a strong relationship. I'm a psychic intuitive and even I don't always know what's on my loved ones' minds all the time! But we can increase our sensitivity to the feelings of others and the energetic currents around them. Much of what's going on with people is unexpressed, so you need to work to tune in to your partner. Take the time to sense the energy of your significant other. Remember that to manifest the relationship quality you want, you have to be present and attentive to the intent of spirit. If you're getting a hit that something's not quite right, ask, "Are you okay?" or "Did I say something wrong?" or "Why do you feel like this?" When you sense someone's energy, you can sense his or her emotions. And by keeping yourself attuned to your partner, you'll experience more of those magical moments when there's silence and you both look at each other at the same time and say "I love you" with your eyes.

In matters of the heart, you must cherish both yours and that of the other person. Love is fragile, and it needs to be respected and taken care of. And think before you speak. My friend Bob says, "Words are like stones—once you throw them out, you can never take them back."

Over the years, our intuitive sense of our significant other can get stronger and stronger. We can feel even more connected at deeper levels. Of course, there will be energy changes in every relationship as we grow and evolve. Part of the joy of a relationship is learning and growing with your partner, and you have to continually refresh your sense of this person if you want a relationship that lasts. As long as you pay attention, your intuition can help you stay tuned in and grow along with your partner.

That is, if you pay attention. The problem is that familiarity breeds not contempt, but comfort, and comfort can breed a tendency to ignore the subtle currents of energy that intuition is designed to pick up. Familiarity can make it easier to sense what's going on with your partner, but it also can make you blind when things are "off." It's almost as if we shut our intuition down because we don't think we need it anymore, now that we think we know this person so well. Once you turn your intuition off, you're losing one of the most intimate connections you can have with a partner. When that unspoken connection goes, you could be growing apart and not realize it.

When people start to take one another for granted, it has far greater negative consequences than you may think. Remember the experiments with rice described by Masaru Emoto, the Japanese scientist? Schoolchildren put out three containers of uncooked rice. Each day they said, "I love you" to one container, "You fool" to a second, and the third they completely ignored. The rice that was ignored rotted faster than the rice that had been told, "You fool." Ignoring our partners and taking them for granted can be more toxic to a relationship than active hate. They may start pushing away from the relationship because they don't feel they are getting the love and attention they need, and then they may look for it elsewhere.

You have to make the time to connect with your partner on all levels. This includes spoken and unspoken communication. How many times do you come home from work and all you want to do is to turn your brain off? Communication is the last thing on your mind. You might feel something's not okay with your partner but you just don't want to "get into it" right now, so you veg out in front of the TV, or eat dinner in silence, or focus on the kids' homework rather than following your intuitive hit that your partner needs you. And your partner says nothing, maybe giving you the silent treatment. You think, *Oh, that just means that they've had a bad day.* But maybe this time a coworker made a pass, or your partner has felt herself attracted to somebody else. Or maybe she's thinking, "You don't appreciate me; when was the last time we talked about something other than the kids?" We get lazy and tired and don't pay attention to our thoughts. Your intuition has warned you, but if you don't follow it up your relationship could be in real trouble. Go the extra distance—it pays off.

Relationship problems show up in many ways. The person you have chosen as your partner may be so similar to you that you start to find him unexciting. Or your partner is your exact opposite, and while you still find him stimulating you're often frustrated by his very different approach to everyday life. Or maybe the love of your life keeps leaving the toothpaste cap off or the toilet seat up or spends too much on coffee every day, and these little things are driving you nuts. Or maybe you just feel the energy is off between you two; there's a sense that you're no longer in sync.

In all these situations I believe intuition can be a relationship-saving skill. It can help you get past your own irritation or blah-ness and sense what's really going on. It also can help you bring to consciousness something you're afraid to face. Clients come to me all the time and say, "I don't know, I feel there's something going on but I can't put my finger on it." In one reading I did on TV, I picked up an L around a woman, then an M, a Mark. I felt there were problems around this man and asked if she was breaking up with him because she thought he was cheating on her. She confirmed it, and that the L was the woman she thought Mark was seeing. "Break it off with him," I advised her. "You'll find someone else who's better for you." My sister Alicia is also really good at picking up on what's happening in her patients' relationships. A man came to see her and said, "I've got to start being nicer. I'm irritable and cranky all the time, I'm just not who I want to be." Alicia replied, "Your wife's upset with you, isn't she? She's a lovely lady, very patient and kind, but she's lost her patience with you." The man was amazed. "You've never met my wife, but you're absolutely right. In fact, she just moved out of the house." Alicia says that when she sees patients often she "just knows" what's going on in their relationships even when they don't tell her.

If you don't sense a problem, or if you sense it intuitively but push the feeling away, often the universe will tip you off in no uncertain terms. A woman might feel something's up with her husband but keep denying the thought—until one day she just happens to hit the redial button on the telephone and up pops the number of another woman. Or a man comes by his wife's store at lunchtime and she's not there, but then he sees her returning from lunch, strolling arm-in-arm with a man. My friend psychic Malcolm Mills did a reading for a woman who was upset because her boyfriend was acting differently. Malcolm told her that his intuition said her boyfriend was gay. The woman got very angry and stormed out. Three weeks later she called him back, contrite—she had walked in on her boyfriend with another man.

The goal of intuition, of course, is to be sensitive to others' feelings even though we're with them all the time. We may have a tendency to take our partners for granted, but we should never abuse that intimacy, trust, or connection. Using your intuition doesn't guarantee you won't have problems, but it can help you discover what's really going on and then communicate at a deep level with your partner. We want to catch prospective relationship problems before they get serious, so you can do something about them—perhaps couples therapy, perhaps one partner seeing a counselor, perhaps a vacation or just a discussion about what's not being said. A problem is a signal that attention needs to be paid; it may be an indication that growth is needed in this particular area of your relationship or your life. Patterns from previous dysfunctional relationships may be showing up and you need to handle them and develop new ways of relating. Remember, pain and problems aren't necessarily a sign that the relationship is done with; they may just be "growing pains" that you need to experience to reach the next level in your love for each other. So many couples tell me about horrible things they've had to endure—tragic accidents, deaths of children or other loved ones, business failures, serious disease—and they became even closer as a result.

I often feel as if people are too quick to give up on their relationships. Don't be one of those who run away too quickly. Use your inner wisdom—logic, common sense, and intuition—to evaluate your problems. Do your best to communicate with your partner on an intuitive as well as verbal level. Remember, there are three sides to every story: the other's side, your side, and the truth! Learn to forgive. Learn to accept apologies from yourself and from others. I can't tell you how many times in readings people who have passed over come through to apologize to the loved ones they left behind. Forgiveness is one of the key lessons we are meant to learn from our relationships, so practice it regularly while your partners are still here.

Every great relationship is not fifty-fifty, but a hundred-hundred; both you and your partner need to give it everything you've got. And if every relationship is a two-way street, make sure you're the first one to cross over to your partner's side of the road. However, if you're giving 110 percent and you're still not happy, then maybe the relationship should end. Relationships end for many reasons: we've grown at a different rate than our partner; we haven't met our partner's needs; or maybe we just realize that what we thought was an intimate relationship should transform into a friendship. Sometimes people stay in a relationship after it has changed to provide a stable family for the children. Relationships are designed to transform us whether we want to or not, and when we change, our energy needs may shift as well.

Sometimes people need to get out of a relationship because it is bad for them. I have a client whose wife was his complete opposite: he was creativity and goodness, and she was chaos and destruction. They were very fiery together, but after a while she started destroying his business. She stole from him; she stole from his business; she manipulated and lied. This good, loving man was forced to develop his intuition to avoid her traps and manipulations. Eventually he was able to free himself from the relationship and move on. I believe that love doesn't mean putting up with someone else's destructive behavior. If someone is destroying himself and you love him, don't enable him! You both need to sober up. As singer Naomi Judd puts it, "You're a victim only once, and after that you're a volunteer."

You may or may not get the signal that it's time for the relationship to end. In some cases, you need the assistance of others to point out to you the correct course of action. I see clients all the time who refuse to recognize the signs that the relationship is over. They're rearranging deck chairs on the *Titanic* while the ship's going down. If they ask me about their relationships, I won't play God and I try to give both sides, but I also have to be truthful. I told one woman, "You're this man's fourth wife and he cheated on three other wives. You caught him cheating in this relationship. Why wouldn't he do it again? It's his MO, his pattern. So if you want to stay with him, you'd better accept that this is who you married and this is what you've asked for." It's so sad when people's infatuations cause them to ignore their logic, common sense, and intuition. In these cases I feel my job is to point out their blind spots and help them learn their lessons as quickly as possible, so they can move out of the relationship and move on to something better. I tell them they can say, "Thank you for all you've given me, it's time to move on."

Like my friend Bob puts it, life is like a bus and you're the driver. Some people will get on, and some people will get off and get back on again. Some people will stay on forever, and others will leave and never return. Don't be too sad that a relationship is over. Cherish that it happened at all. Relationships come into our lives to help us learn and grow, and that learning may include the acceptance of the end of the partnership. The fact that our relationships end is part of the inevitable cycle of birth, growth, and death. No loss is ever easy, and it's inevitable to feel pain and sorrow with the loss of a relationship, no matter how it concludes. If we approach the end of a relationship looking for the lessons to be learned; if we can see this as one more stage in the great cycle of life; if we can experience the pain fully while acknowledging the possibility that this loss may be the opening for the universe to bring something even better into our lives; then we are using relationships as they were designed, as a path to growth as well as a reminder of the power of love.

Love Never Dies

I once read for a woman named Teresa, who had lost her husband a year and a half earlier. The two of them had been inseparable, doing everything together, and now she said it was as if her legs had been amputated. She hadn't worked since his death. Her children, friends, and neighbors were all worried sick. Her husband had built and decorated the home where they had lived for twenty years, and she had put it on the market, but she didn't feel comfortable doing so. Yet she was in such pain from staying in the house, which her husband had built and decorated, that she could barely function.

In the reading, Teresa's husband, Bill, came through clear and strong. "He's already given you many signs of his presence," I told her. "Tell me about the flowers." Teresa said that when her husband died, she and her children had taken his ashes to Portugal because he loved that part of the world. When they returned home they found his favorite flower, which he himself had planted in the garden, in full bloom. A flower that normally comes out in May or June had blossomed in February.

Teresa and Bill had owned two cars, one big and one small, and she decided to trade in both of them for a midsize model. When she came to pick up the car, the salesperson said, "We always give our customers flowers when they purchase a car from us. Normally it's tulips, but we ran out. We hope you like these instead," and he gave her a big bouquet of her husband's favorite flower.

As the reading continued I had a sense of Bill's ashes in the living room of the house. "You kept his ashes in the house for a few weeks, and they kept moving, didn't they?" I asked.

Teresa was amazed—even though the kids swore they never touched the container, the ashes had all of a sudden appeared in the bathroom. "You know why? He decorated the entire house, except the bathroom. He's telling you he wants you to change the house to your taste," I told her. "Your husband is giving you many signs and signals. All you need to do is listen to your intuition and you'll find comfort knowing he's with you still."

At the end of the reading, Teresa's face looked completely different. She was happier, lighter, more at peace. She went home and slept for ten hours straight, the longest she had slept since her husband died. She was able to work again. Her children were delighted to see the change in their mother. She also decided to stay in her home. When she threw away the For Sale sign in her yard, the neighbors threw her a party.

Love is the strongest energy that exists. From serving as the bridge between this world and the next for thirty years, I can attest that the energy of love never dies, and our relationships with the people we care about will continue beyond death. Love is the bridge to the other side; the spirits that speak through me do so because they are connected through love with those who are still here. The stronger the loving bond, the stronger the connection. So many husbands, wives, mothers, fathers, friends come through because they want to let those who are here know that their love is unchanged and eternal, and they will be there to welcome us when it's our turn to pass over. As I said to one young girl whose grandmother had died a month earlier, "Your grandfather's name was Peter, wasn't it? Well, just like St. Peter at the pearly gates, Peter met your grandmother and embraced her when she passed."

The energy of love is powerful and healing on the spirit plane as well as here, and we can send our love to those who have passed over, simply by thinking of them. But please, don't wait until your loved ones have passed to let them know how much you care. Say "I love you" while they are still alive. Embrace them before they leave the earth plane. When they go, you will remember every embrace, every expression of love—and so will they. These moments of shared love are the real treasures that never rust or fade; they are the only things we can take with us when we die. Build up your treasures on earth, my friends, by giving and sharing love. Use your inner wisdom to attract, choose, and nurture your loving connections with others. Don't let any relationship problems fester or go ignored; get therapy and get things handled. If necessary, let relationships go gracefully and be open to the love the universe always wants to send your way. And know that your love for friends, family, and lovers will endure past death and provide a bridge that connects you with them forever.

7

Tuning In to and Turning On
Your Sexual Energy

*Sex is one of the nine reasons for reincarnation. The other eight
are unimportant.*

—Henry Miller

Sex can be one of the deepest connections we have with
another human being. In moments of intimacy we feel we
are united with a partner; we might even feel we can read our
partner's mind or emotions. Sex is also one of the most powerful energy forces in our lives, driving our behavior and our
relationships. The energy of sex is so great that cultures and
religions throughout the years have suppressed it, celebrated
it, and tried to sublimate it. In fact, some psychics actually
pull energy from their sexual center (the lower two chakras)
to "charge" their intuitive batteries. But whether you're an
"anything goes" person, a "nothing doing" one, or anywhere
in between, you cannot ignore this vital part of yourself.

Many of my clients ask questions directly related to their

sex lives. As an intuitive, it's pretty easy for me to pick up on whether someone is straight, gay, or bisexual, happy or unhappy, faithful or fooling around. But even if we don't acknowledge it, almost everyone has a sixth sense when it comes to sex. Much of the time when a client asks me a question related to an intimate partner, all I'm doing is confirming what the client already senses intuitively.

Unfortunately, when it comes to a strong sexual attraction, the three components of inner wisdom—logic, common sense, and intuition—can go right out the window. We become lost in the "drive" part of the sex drive as we're swept along by our needs. Any vestige of common sense is overridden by desire and wishful thinking. Recently I had a client who had broken up with his girlfriend awhile ago, and then she e-mailed him out of the blue. When he called for a reading, he told me, "It's clear I'm not going to end up with her, but I just want you to tell me—will I have sex with her again?" He was completely obsessed by his sexual connection with this woman.

Manifesting sexual energy is relatively easy, because it is a common biological drive. In *The Secret* a counselor tells an artistic young playboy how to manifest the three dates a week he wants. She tells him to visualize, even paint, himself with lots of beautiful women. Then, when he says he wants a relationship with just one woman, she tells him to literally paint himself in a touching, romantic scene with just one woman he adores. Within a few months, he is engaged and deeply in love, and loved in return. Sexual energy is a powerful tool when melded with the power of intuition.

Adepts and masters from traditions all over the world show us that the energy of sex can be channeled and used to create deeper connections with ourselves, our partners, and universal energy as well. When you apply what these masters have to teach, you can use your inner wisdom to help you:

- Attract your ideal partner

- Protect yourself from energy "vampires" and those who would use the power of attraction to harm you

- Join with your partner in fulfilling, delicious, ecstatic sex

- Use sexual energy as a path to connection with a higher level of spiritual consciousness

The Energy of Attraction

Attraction, sexual energy, chemistry—they all come from the ability to sense the energy of another human being and to have them sense ours. You walk by someone and think, *This person's really hot.* You make eye contact with a person across the room at a party. You pick up on the energy of another and something in it causes a little stir inside, a resonance, a recognition of the potential for connection. In some cases, this recognition is like a lightning bolt—that "love at first sight" instant rapport. I read about a woman who noticed a fellow standing on a crowded train platform in Pennsylvania Station in New York City. He looked like what he was, a poor writer who worked in an art postcard factory. He got on the same train she did and sat opposite her. They chatted for a while and then he gave her a postcard that showed two lovers kissing—and she felt as if she had been struck by lightning. The moment before she had felt nothing but friendship for this comparative stranger, but in the next second, she was completely smitten and felt totally attracted to him. Two months later they were living together, and they were married within the year.

I believe we're attracted to what we want in our lives, whether it's more of what we have (in which case, we're attracted to people who are like us) or what we don't have but would like (for example, a "good" girl may want the excitement and danger that a "bad" boy represents). However, I also believe that the law of attraction can be triggered by many different factors. First and foremost, our own energy affects what we are attracted to and who is attracted to us. If you're feeling on top of the world, what kind of people do you like to be around? Other happy people, of course. On the other hand, if you're miserable, those happy people usually make you angry—you'd rather be around people who sympathize with you or who feel as lousy as you do. That's why you first must get your own emotional energy into line before you start looking for a relationship. Knowing yourself; staying in touch with your own energy, your thoughts, your biochemistry; and trying to be as balanced as you possibly can—psychologically, emotionally, and physically—are absolutely essential for attracting a healthy partner.

When it comes to sexual energy and attraction, it's very important to use your intuition to pick up any warnings of a possibly dangerous relationship. Attraction has two sides; when we're in the throes of attraction we blind ourselves to the warnings our intuition may be trying to provide. In today's world of Internet and speed dating, where our potential partners may come from the other side of the world rather than from our own neighborhood, and we can learn more about people while knowing less about their real character, it's more important than ever that we try to push our sexual energy and attraction aside, use our inner wisdom to evaluate our partners, and then listen to any warnings or positive signs we receive.

These messages can come from our inner promptings or from friends and family. Sometimes our own intuition isn't quite tuned in to a prospective partner because we're being blinded by our rules about what he or she should look like or be like. Someone might not be your type but his soul is good and he would cherish you. Your friends and family often can see these people more clearly than you can at first. They also can see problems faster than you can in some cases. If others encourage you or warn you, evaluate what you're getting from them. If the warning or encouragement comes from inside you, evaluate it, too, but make sure to heed your intuitive hit. It could be that you're being warned about possible pain and yet your lesson is to go through the pain and learn from it. It could be that your lesson is to learn to listen to your inner warnings! Whenever you feel uneasy, check in and ask for clarity, surround yourself with a white light of protection, and if you need to get out of the situation, do so immediately. Better that you lose a possible relationship than be hurt or worse. It also could be your lesson is to look beyond the surface and see a wonderful soul who wants to love you. Intuition can help us see the truth of another person. Let yourself be open to the signs the universe wants to give you, to lead you to a loving partner.

Unfortunately, once you've given in to the sexual attraction of another, you can get to the point where you're literally addicted to a partner's bad energy. I told one client, "You're absolutely hooked on this guy even though he's no good. He's like heroin or cocaine for you, and just like a drug, he's going to drag you down unless you break your addiction." Sexual attraction can make us deaf to what our intuition is screaming in our ears. Breaking away from this kind of sexual addiction can be very difficult, but it is essential for our physical, emotional, and psychic well-being. It's far better to sense the potential for addiction early and avoid the relationship altogether. If you're caught up in it, leave immediately. The longer you stay in, the tougher it can be to get out without some kind of karmic residue (and even more pain and suffering).

In most cases, however, attraction, the sexual charge between people, is simply a calling of one being to another, with the goal of coming together in joy. Attraction feels so good because we are opening ourselves to love, which is what we are made of and what we were born to give and receive. Attraction is usually the universe's sign that it wants to give us a greater, more loving, more abundant life. We manifest love in our lives by being ready and saying yes when the gift is offered.

Sexual Orientation: Choice or Karma?

Not too long ago I did a reading for a very strong, wonderful woman, Roberta. Roberta was a transsexual—born a man but feeling as if he was a woman inside. He had married a woman and had children, but after several years decided to undergo the operations that would make him female. His parents had died before he could explain his sexuality to them, so he had come to me hoping to communicate with them. I was able to reach his parents and his deceased sister. I told Roberta, "Everyone lives more than one lifetime on this earth, and we come back as different genders. Sometimes the lifetimes we've had before affect us; sometimes we come back physically as one gender and emotionally and spiritually as another. That's why there are masculine men, feminine men, masculine women, and feminine women. I think that's why so many people are confused about their sexuality—their desires are different from their anatomy this time around. My feeling is that your spirit is female but you came into a male body. It must have been terrible to live with that. But your parents see and understand now. Your mother also wants me to talk about your wife. Your wife and children will support you through this."

I have many clients who are gay or bisexual. Some are very comfortable and open with their sexual orientation, while others try to keep it under wraps. However, it's pretty easy to pick up intuitively on sexual energy, even when someone is trying to hide it. When we're not happy with ourselves or we're confused about what we're feeling, that turmoil is very evident to an intuitive.

A lot of people don't necessarily have problems about their sexual orientation, but they do have conflicts about letting others know. But just like Roberta, when we feel we need to hide a part of who we are from the people we love, it creates enormous tension and pain inside. I believe the best thing we can do for ourselves in that kind of situation is to get help, perhaps through therapy, so we can accept ourselves. That's usually the first step to helping those around us to accept us, too.

When souls recognize each other and there's karma to be played out, I find that social standards often can go out the window. The key to all of this is for people to know and accept themselves for who they are at their core. I'm not talking about accepting any tendency to hurt others or to be hurt by them. Most of us can tell when our choices are hurting other people physically, psychologically, or emotionally. But when it comes to our choice of partners or sexual orientation, we need to be secure within ourselves about our sexuality and have confidence about our relationships, making sure we're happy with who and what we are. I've read for gay, straight, and bisexual people, and the truth is that in relationships there's not much of a difference. Relationships are about loving and respecting each other, communicating clearly, and working on the relationship to keep it healthy and alive.

Connecting with Your Partner

The drive of sexual energy is to connect with a partner. When that connection is healthy and reciprocal, the union of the energy of both parties can create something greater than the sum of two parts. Anyone who has been in the first flush of love or sexual attraction knows the tension produced by coming together and being apart. We walk down the street and we still can feel the caress of a lover, or we catch a whiff of a particular scent in the air and immediately long for the lover's presence. We hear "our" song and imagine holding our beloved in our arms. This sensual energy expands our awareness of all of our senses. That's why, when we are in a passionate relationship, we experience greater enjoyment of sensual foods, aromas, physical sensations, sights, and sounds.

Conversely, enjoyment of our senses can help us connect better with our own sensual energy and thus with a partner. Think about eating some of the finest caviar in the world, or sharing a glass of superb wine or brandy. Imagine the feel of satin against your body, or running your hand over your partner's silk robe. Perhaps you smell the particular fragrance your partner wears, or incense or flowers placed in your bedroom. Maybe there is music playing, something slow and sensual, or strongly rhythmic, with a strong bass or drumbeat. (Vibration and rhythm are very stimulating to the sexual core of the body.) Sharing any of these experiences with a partner will help you both tune in to the same sensual, sexual energy and join at an even more profound level.

I also believe that focusing on the sensual aspects of sex will help you stay in the moment and keep the sexual energy flowing between you and your partner. How many of us have found our minds wandering during sex? (Be honest—it happens to everyone.) We can have the best intentions and really love our partners, but if we've had a bad day at the office or with the kids, if we're just plain tired or have something weighing on our minds, it's not surprising that we can lose focus on our partners for a moment or even longer. And because sex is as much about a connection of energy as it is about a connection of flesh, our partners will usually sense when our focus shifts away from the moment. So when your mind starts to wander, pull it back by noticing something sensual. Don't start thinking *I should be paying attention;* that will keep you in your head rather than your body. Just see or hear or feel something you like that will bring you into the present.

Tuning in on a sensual level also will help you keep the sexual energy alive in your relationship. Studies indicate that our biochemistry programs us to be sexually attracted to the same person for about two years. After that the chemicals that create that immediate sexual urge start to diminish. That's why it's so important to focus on the energy of sex and sensuality rather than expecting it just to be there. Learning to be in the present moment, to focus on the sensual aspects of an encounter, to connect intuitively as well as physically with your partner, will help you keep the energetic connection between the two of you strong and vital.

Do you remember what those first few weeks and months of a sexual relationship feel like—the excitement, the freshness, the sense of discovery with each other? I've found that when that sense of freshness wears off and sex becomes mechanical, partners start to seek fulfillment outside of the relationship, or even seek another relationship entirely. Perhaps, as those studies show, we're only biochemically attracted to someone for about two years, but that doesn't mean we don't still love our partner and feel connected to him or her at a very deep level. One of the ways we seem to compensate for this hormonal "drop-off" is through fantasy. Most people have fantasized their partner is someone else—Brad Pitt or Angelina Jolie or some other "hot" celebrity. Rather than seeing this as disrespect and lack of passion, I agree with my friend Malcolm Mills that fantasy can be a healthy addition to any relationship.

Malcolm, who has studied intuition and sexual energy, reminds us that essentially, sex should be play for adults. "A lot of cheating has to do with a man or woman being unable to find the fantasy within the marriage and so they go outside," he says. "Role-playing can make sex fun again for couples who are burned out on the same old, same old." Malcolm tells a story of two people who had been married for a long time and who constantly invented new identities for themselves as part of their sex life. The wife would go out to dinner by herself and sit alone at a table, and ten minutes later the husband would come in and pretend to be a stranger who wanted to pick her up. They'd try on different roles and use costumes to enhance the sexual experience for them both. Malcolm says that this couple is one of the happiest he has ever seen.

It's important for all of us to recognize the power of sexual, sensual energy. If we bring to our sensual connections with a partner a desire to love, to bond, to be close, to experience mutual ecstasy, then our sexual energy sways to the positive side. On the other hand, if we use our sexual energy, or withhold it, in order to dominate, to hurt, to coerce, or to repay supposed (or real) slights, then we turn this powerful force on its head and create negative energy as a result.

You also need to recognize your sexual boundaries and those of your partner. Different people have different rules and requirements when it comes to sexual activities, the number of sexual partners, sex outside of the relationship, and so on. Some swingers can't be happy unless they are having sex with a lot of people; others use drugs like Ecstasy to enhance their sexual experience. Still others may find themselves slipping into sexual addiction. If a swinger is in a relationship with someone who isn't into free-for-all sex, obviously this can cause problems in the relationship. It's very important for people to recognize that whenever sex is a shared activity, they need to take their partners' rules and boundaries into account. Sex is a merging of energy between partners, and it requires respect as well as love.

Sharing sexual energy is one of the most wonderful things on earth, and sometimes can be dangerous as well. When you are engaged sexually with someone your energy is vulnerable. Choosing a sex partner who has your best interests at heart on all levels will keep you protected. Once your sexual energy merges with another you are taking on his energy as well, so you want your partner to be pure and balanced in every way. If he is not a pure soul you may be inviting unwanted vibrations into your psyche and energy field. If you feel that the sexual energy between you and your partner is taking a turn you don't like, talk to him about it, and if you feel threatened or possibly open to injury in any way, get help—either by leaving the relationship or by asking your partner to seek professional help.

Sex is like chocolate—a wonderful, delicious, sensual experience that is even better when shared with someone you love. Like chocolate, there are many different varieties and iterations of sex, and not every variety is to everyone's taste. I may love caramel while my lover hates it. I may want to eat chocolate three or four times a day; my lover may be completely satiated with one really great chocolate a day or even one a week. And if I can't get enough chocolate no matter how much I eat, then I need to recognize I have a problem. But when you and a partner decide on what chocolate you want to eat, when you want to eat it, and how much chocolate is to both of your tastes, then your palate will never be satiated and you can enjoy your chocolate together for many years to come.

Connecting with Higher Energy

Many couples will tell you that it's during or after sex that they feel most closely attuned with their partner, almost as if they could read the other's mind or pick up on their emotions. That's because sexual energy connects us not only on a physical and emotional level but on an intuitive level as well.

And this intuitive connection also can form a bridge to higher levels of energy and tune us in to higher realms. That connection with higher energy is recognized by many religious and spiritual traditions. Rabbi Nachmanides, a Jewish scholar who lived in twelfth-century Spain and who contended that our human nature is as divine as our soul, wrote in his book *The Sacred Letter,* "When a man cleaves to his wife in holiness, the divine presence is manifested. In the mystery of man and woman, there is God."

The classic path for using sexual energy to connect with the divine is tantra. (I don't claim to be an expert in this area, but I do have a great appreciation for how tantra approaches the energy of sex.) In tantra, the partners come together with the goal of using the sexual energy to arouse the kundalini, the spiritual energy that lies coiled like a snake at the base of the spine. When tantric practices awaken the kundalini, it moves up the spine, through the energy centers of the body (chakras) and out into the universe, allowing both partners to reach union with divine bliss. Tantric sex originated in the Hindu tradition and is seen by both Buddhists and Taoists as a way of reaching enlightenment. While some can follow the path of meditation and self-control, tantra is a path that can be embraced by those who possess great passion. Both paths are seen as equally valid. As Mantak Chia, a well-known Eastern master of energy, says, "You can either pray a hundred thousand hours or you can consciously guide the sexual energy up the spine."

While many people in the West know tantra from the poses of the Kama Sutra, in reality tantra is only about energy—tuning in to your own sexual energy, which is a manifestation of the divine, and joining that energy to that of your partner with the goal of complete merging with the divine. This energy is nurtured in every moment of a tantric encounter. Unlike the common Western view, which holds orgasm as the most important moment of sex, tantric sex views orgasm as optional or something to be delayed as the sexual energy is allowed to subside and build again so it can move higher up the spine. In tantra, we connect the physical body with the energetic body, and sex becomes both a physical and a spiritual experience.

Some of the practices described by tantric experts include:

- Prolonged foreplay that uses all five senses to connect you with your partner

- Creating a sacred space for sex using lighting, oils, foods, textures, drinks, fragrances, and more

- Connecting through the eyes before, during, and after the physical joining

- Extending the sexual experience beyond the genitals to include every part of the body

- Spending hours instead of minutes for each encounter

- Using the breath to harmonize your energy with your partner's

- Visualizing the movement of energy throughout the energy centers of the body

• Worshipping your lover as a god or goddess and receiving the same attention from your partner. In fact, tantra's goal is to become god and goddess, divine lovers, in the act of universal bliss

Remember that sexual energies are not to be taken lightly; they are a powerful force and can make life a heaven or a hell. And since sexual energies tend to obliterate two of the three components of inner wisdom—logic and common sense—it's more important than ever that we tap into the power of our intuition and intention to direct this force toward our higher good. As mature adults, it's our responsibility to use our sexual energy to connect, to love, to enlighten, to raise our consciousness and that of our partner, so that this most powerful force can be a vehicle that allows us to unite ourselves with the highest level of goodness and love.

8

Parenting and Inner Wisdom

Our birth is but a sleep and a forgetting:
The Soul that rises with us, our life's Star,
Hath had elsewhere its setting,
And cometh from afar:
Not in entire forgetfulness,
And not in utter nakedness,
But trailing clouds of glory do we come
From God, who is our home:
Heaven lies about us in our infancy!

—William Wordsworth

Most parents will say they often feel an intuitive, wordless connection with their children. Just as children can tell when Mommy or Daddy is upset even when parents try to pretend otherwise, parents innately know when their children are hurt, frustrated, angry, or unhappy—even when those children may be out of sight. For example, I read a story of a woman who was writing a letter to her daughter, who was away at college. Suddenly, the mother felt an unexplained, burning pain in her right hand. About an hour later she received a call from her daughter, who had burned her right hand in a chemistry lab experiment at that same moment!

In some ways I feel a little odd talking about intuitive parenting because I've never been a parent. However, I'm fortunate that both my sisters, Elaine and Alicia, and their husbands are amazing parents. Because my sisters are nine and thirteen years older than me, I've had the chance to observe them as parents since I was eight. (In school that year, for show and tell I said, "My sister's having a baby today," and no one believed me.) I've been around my nieces and nephews from the moment they were born. As a teenager I was a built-in babysitter, and I've always been a very hands-on aunt and now great-aunt. I love my nieces and nephews and their kids.

I'm fortunate that my sister Alicia is not only a parent and a great therapist but was also a kindergarten teacher and school psychologist for many years. Alicia counsels mothers, fathers, and children as part of her practice in Michigan. She's one of the most intuitive people I know, and she uses her extensive counseling background, her own sixth sense, and most of all, her enormous sense of compassion and empathy to work miracles with her clients. Alicia and I have worked together in many situations where parents and children need extra help getting over trauma or discovering the roots of their problems.

I remember one case in particular where both Alicia and I were needed. A few years ago, a couple from Ann Arbor, Michigan, brought their nine-year-old son to see Alicia. Their little boy was agoraphobic and had obsessive-compulsive disorder. He wouldn't go out of the house or even into certain rooms. He would wash his hands and wipe them until they were raw. This poor little boy had been in treatment at the psychiatry department at the University of Michigan, but he wasn't getting any better.

The dad was a research scientist and Mom was a nutritionist, and neither had much belief in anything outside traditional medicine, but one day the mother read Brian Weiss's book *Many Lives, Many Masters,* which is about past lives. She had an intuitive hit that this might help her son, so she called Brian Weiss's office in Florida, and they referred her to Alicia, who has been doing past-life regression therapy for many years. The parents brought their son to see Alicia, and she had several regression sessions with him. The little boy was doing much better for a while, but then he relapsed. At that point Alicia asked the parents if they'd be willing to talk to me. Luckily, they agreed.

I told them there was a spirit in their house, the spirit of a man who had been involved with pornography. (After this session, the parents searched their house and found a stash of pornography hidden in the attic.) Without meaning to, this spirit was frightening the little boy and needed to be released if the child was to get well. I suggested that these people return to my sister to help the boy release the spirit. Alicia did a spirit-release therapy, and as soon as the session was over, the little boy started to get better. Alicia continued to treat him, and he made rapid progress. Today he's a senior in college, healthy and happy and completely normal.

All parents want what's best for their children, and I applaud these two parents for listening to their intuition and being open to other avenues of help when the traditional ones didn't succeed. I believe that there was a reason that these parents came to Alicia for help: their intuitive knowing of what their son truly needed. If you listen to your heart as well as your head, you will always be a better parent. Intuitive parents can give their children both roots and wings, showing them how to be in the world while allowing them to express all the beauty, joy, and creativity that is every child's birthright.

Unfortunately, far too many parents ignore their own intuitive sense of what's right for their children, relying instead on reports from teachers, child-rearing books, advice from well-meaning friends and relatives, and their own hazy memories of how they themselves were parented. They also sometimes forget that the child in front of them is a unique soul who has been entrusted to them to bring up in the world. The most important thing parents can do is appreciate that soul's uniqueness and tune in intuitively to how that uniqueness expresses itself.

I was lucky enough to have had intuitive parents who appreciated my own psychic gifts. When I was four years old and told my father the lady at the grocery store cheated us, he didn't shush me. Instead, he counted his change. Throughout my childhood and teenage years my parents supported me with great love and understanding. Because of them, I have been able to express my own gifts and talents fully. And because of them, I teach this work in the hope that all parents will give the same opportunities to the children who have been entrusted to their care.

Our Children Choose Us

I believe the children in our lives choose to be part of our families. There are spirits around each of us waiting to be born, and they whisper in our thoughts, "I want you to be my mommy and daddy." For whatever reason—karma from past lives, relationships that need to be worked through, lessons to be learned by both child and parent—our children decide that we are the ones to bring them into physical form. Saying yes to the request of these spirits creates (or re-creates) a relationship that is like no other, a bond that lasts throughout this lifetime and beyond.

We all come from the same place originally—from the energy of love before we're born—and children teach us how to connect to that universal love because they have visited its source more recently. When you spend any time around a child, you know there is something special about that time of life. There is a freshness and innocence about most children. By their very presence in our lives, children remind us of the divine wisdom, goodness, and love that lie at the core of each of us.

And oh my, are children intuitive! Children are so pure and unclouded by adults' ideas and notions that the universe can bring information through them. Not only do children read situations around them and speak the truth without editing their words, but they are truthful, pure vessels for intuitive information as well.

Right from the beginning, there is often an intuitive bond between mother and child. This is not surprising, since children are connected to their mothers through nine months of intimate physical closeness even before they are born. Many women will tell you that a child inside them is clearly its own person with its own likes and dislikes. In fact, it's possible that the cravings pregnant women experience are a direct reflection of the preferences of the baby inside them. A pregnant woman who can't stand to eat meat, for example, may find that the baby she's carrying chooses to be a vegetarian later in life.

After children are born, they communicate their wants, needs, and desires without words (and without crying in many cases, despite what parents of a newborn may think). Every mother knows that when she's upset, her baby will most likely be upset, too, and when she's feeling calm, the baby will calm down. Instinctively babies and children know what the people around them are feeling, whether their care-takers are upset, angry, happy, or serene. There are even studies that show many babies know intuitively that their mothers or caretakers are getting ready to leave, even if all leaving prepara-tions are taking place out of sight.

As children continue to grow, their intuition shows up in many surprising ways. It's a common experience, for example, to observe twins who are closely attuned to each other—one twin can feel when the other twin is hurt or in distress, even if that twin is not physically present. There also are many cases where brothers and sisters can pick up on the emotions of their siblings. For example, maybe Mom and Dad are trying to fig-ure out why their one-year-old daughter is crying when their four-year-old son walks in and says, "She wants her dolly." Mom hands her daughter the doll, and immediately the little girl stops crying.

Intuition in children also shows up in their sensitivity to the emotions of others. For the most part, children are very empathic and they tune in to the emotions of their playmates very quickly. If you've ever seen young children try to com-fort someone else, you know exactly what I mean—their care and love are so palpable and genuine. This empathic, intuitive connection has two sides, however, because it means children also are deeply affected by the negative emotions of the adults around them. They are like lightning rods for any tension or discord in a family, demonstrating emotional difficulties in times of stress.

As a family therapist, my sister Alicia sees so many kids who are "acting out" because their parents are unhappy, angry, or upset with each other. "Even though the parents may try to hide their problems, they can't because their kids can sense it," she says. "I tell parents, if you want a happy child, get yourself happy. Because kids know when things aren't going right."

The best thing parents can do for their children is to care for them *and* care for their relationship with each other. If you're having problems, work them out. If you need to separate, for goodness' sake, do your best to respect each other in the process. Otherwise, you're setting up your intuitive children for a lot of conflict and unhappiness. A very smart young woman once proposed that when parents divorce the kids should keep the house and the parents should have to share custody by moving in and out rather than the other way around! Parents need to realize that they have signed up for an eternal relationship when they have kids, and it's not one they can get out of with divorce or even death. Your children are your children no matter what—and you need to hold that responsibility very highly in your heart and mind.

Parents' Intuition

Children can be old souls in young bodies, wise beyond their years in universal love. However, they come into this world unprepared for its demands. As adults, the job of parents is to teach children how to adapt to the world this time around, and to start them on the journey of discovery and learning that is the reason the children chose to be born.

Again, as a nonparent I am not an expert, but from watching many parents in my lifetime, I believe that parents have to tune in to their own intuitive sense, their gut sense of what's needed. However, as my sister Alicia says, "Some parents are afraid to let themselves really listen to their inner knowing. They're afraid they may need to change something and they're comfortable with the status quo, even if their kids are not." Good parents must learn to read the smallest signs in their children's demeanor, picking up on the eddies and currents of their emotions, and then be willing to give their children the emotional support they need.

It's very important to support the healthy development of your children in all areas, including your child's intuition. Studies of child development tell us that the first parts of the brain to develop are the intuitive, feeling areas; these are already rich in neural connections during our childhood years. The very last parts of the brain to develop fully are the frontal lobes, which are responsible for governing our actions and behavior. Unfortunately, when it comes to a child's intuition, adults act as surrogate frontal lobes, telling the child to stop lying, that their intuitions are wrong, and that their fantastic dreams and thoughts are unreal. Is it any wonder that by the time we're grown up most of us have suppressed our natural sixth sense?

Certainly parents have to act as "frontal lobes" at times to keep the child safe. But we also need to validate and appreciate the expressions of a child's intuitive nature. As parents you should always be open and accepting of the experiences your children share with you. Do you listen to your children's dreams? Sometimes their dreams are communications from loved ones on the other side, or perhaps indications of what actions the child may want to take in a certain situation. Do you hear their tales of what happened while they were playing or at school and tell them, "That could never happen; I'm sure you just imagined that"? If your child tells you about an experience that seems far-fetched to you but may be an intuitive experience, hear him out. Never tell him, "That's silly!" or "That's impossible!" or "That couldn't really happen." Certainly children may be making things up, but you can use your own intuition to help you discover what are tall tales and what are actual narrations of experience.

Let your children express themselves fully and accept their intuitive experiences without judgment. If you feel fear or anger, your emotions will be communicated to your child even if you don't say the words. We've all seen movies where children can "see dead people" or tune in to the energies of spirits or places. Unfortunately, most of the time these films are designed to scare the heck out of the adults and children who may be watching them. The absolute worst thing we can do for children is to make them afraid of their own natural intuitive gifts, even if those gifts mean they can sense spirits or energies. Intuitive experiences are simply due to their being able to use another sense—their innate sixth sense. Some children are more intuitive than others, but they all have a baseline intuitive nature. Honor their perceptions and hunches. Listen to their dreams. Take the time to appreciate your children and their intuitive gifts, and you will be repaid by watching them come fully into their potential.

I believe one of the primary ways children's intuitive sense shows up is through their "imaginary playmates." Such playmates are part of childhood for many kids, and luckily today adults are taught to simply treat these invisible friends as a normal phase of the child's development. But such invisible playmates actually may be spirit guides or guardian angels communicating directly to the intuitive child. The best thing adults can do with invisible playmates is not to pooh-pooh their existence, thereby denying the child's experience of his or her intuition. To make sure the spirit is a benevolent one, teach your child how to put white light around him- or herself—if the spirit is good, it will exist comfortably in the white light. And treat the invisible friend in exactly the same way you treat other friends and playmates. As a parent you care about who your child spends time with, right? You want him or her to be around others who provide good company and a good example. A good spirit will have the child's best interests at heart and can give good advice, encouragement, and protection. If you feel the advice is leading your child astray, put your own white light around your child and tell the spirit to leave. We control spirits, they don't control us.

In truth, every time we teach our kids to stay away from people who "feel funny" or who give them a "bad feeling," we are helping them develop their sixth sense. One of the best protections we can offer our children is to teach them this inner knowing of good and bad, helpful and unhelpful, safe and dangerous. You can do this by showing them how to do a gut check in every situation. Do they feel light and happy inside when they are in the situation, or does something make them feel cold, heavy, or scared? Or are they feeling light and happy but there's also another little niggling feeling telling them to be careful? Warnings come in many different forms, and spirits can look fair and still feel foul. You want your children to use their inborn sense of good and bad to keep them safe from danger. When you help your kids recognize the promptings of their own inner awareness, you will be giving them an invaluable level of protection that will care for them even when you're not around.

One of the side benefits of teaching your kids about doing gut checks early will show up when your child becomes a teenager. By definition the teenage years are filled with confusion and exploding hormones, with low impulse control coupled with greater opportunities for temptation. As a parent, the best thing you can do is to help your kids develop their intuition before their hormones throw everything out of whack. Teach your children how to read a situation and feel danger before it happens. Most people know both intellectually and intuitively the difference between right and wrong. Show your teenagers the importance of sensing whether something is right or wrong, safe or dangerous, and making smart decisions. Certainly you may not stop them from doing some truly stupid things—after all, they're teenagers—but you may help keep them safe in the long run.

As parents, we want to manifest the best possible outcomes for our teens, and part of the very process of adolescence is learning to use the law of attraction. By setting the example of a parent who manifests love, joy, people, things, opportunities, peace, and so on in your own life, you expose a child of any age to the gift of intuition and a grounded awareness of the dramatic power of the law of attraction. Even if you are just learning these principles now, it's never too late for a child of any age to benefit from your example.

Part of your responsibility to your children is to be aware of when they need extra psychological help. Intuition is not a shield for your children any more than it is a shield for you. If your child is having trouble coping, if you're listening to her and supporting her to your best ability and your child is still not happy or having problems, get help—for her and for yourself if necessary. Sometimes we can't be aware of all the pressures children are under, and they need someone else to talk to, to help them work things out. A good therapist who can tune in to a child's needs can be a huge support in times of trouble. Interview different therapists first, use your own intuition to check out the therapist, and finally, let your child see the therapist a few times to make sure they're in tune. Partner with the therapist to give your child the support he or she needs to take care of the challenges he or she is facing.

Children and Learning

All children learn intuitively and creatively. They pick things up from their environment in every way possible, without thinking about it or working to absorb their lessons. They learn from metaphors and stories, from art and drawing, from play and communication with others. They learn from the emotions of playmates and adults. Before they ever set foot in a school, children have absorbed massive amounts of learning simply by being themselves.

And then comes school . . . where they are expected to be

like all the other children, to learn in a prescribed manner, to fit into the model of how lessons are presented and according to a specific timetable. If they succeed in squashing their own individuality and conform to the rules, they are rewarded. If for whatever reason their particular learning style or stage of development isn't in sync with their classmates, they are punished—maybe not physically, but with emotional consequences of adult disapproval, concern, perhaps even anger. Is it a wonder that many kids nowadays would rather play video games than go to school?

And at school the kids themselves can be as judgmental as the adults. Peer pressure is something that every child has to deal with—especially when his intuitive gift or talent sets him apart. I remember all too well being thought "weird" by some of the popular kids in high school, not just because I had these flashes of intuition, but also simply because I was in the school choir and performed in musicals. As parents, teachers, and mentors we need to do our best to help our kids understand that it's more important to be individuals, do what they love, and follow their gifts instead of trying to live up to any ridiculous rules that the popular kids decree. That's a lesson our children need to learn early, because all through life people will try to tell them what's acceptable and what's not, and it will be up to them to live according to what they believe is important for them. Children who have a strong intuitive sense especially will need to follow their gifts no matter what others say or believe.

As a former kindergarten teacher, Alicia has definite opinions on what children need so they can excel in school. She believes that all great teachers are intuitive and empathic, more interested in helping each child learn than in group results.

Alicia states, "Every child wants to do well, but teachers and parents have to meet the child where he or she is, not where they want the child to be. I used to call it 'tuning in to channel David,' or whatever the child's name is. When you meet each child at his or her own level, it's much easier to know what will be the best way to teach that particular child."

Unfortunately, in today's classrooms where many teachers are expected to manage twenty to thirty children at a time, such individualized attention is almost impossible. But great teachers still try to use their own intuitive sense of what a child needs in the moment. Parents—poor, overworked, and overscheduled souls that they are—also need to pay close attention to their children's progress; not to berate the child or the teacher if there are problems, but so parents can do their best to discover what kind of support the child needs in order to learn.

This is a challenge, because today far too much emphasis is placed on every child hitting the same benchmarks at the same time when it comes to school. If your kid hasn't mastered the alphabet and basic mathematics by the time he or she leaves kindergarten, then horrors! That could mean he or she won't get into a good college when the time comes. But while poor little Johnny is having trouble telling his letters apart, he's drawing beautiful, freeform pictures of airplanes and angels and telling Mom and Dad about how he helped a friend who skinned his knee. Little Johnny's empathy and creativity are well developed, and isn't that important, too? The best thing we can do for our children is to notice their strengths at every level of development, praise them for their accomplishments no matter how small, and get creative ourselves in the ways we help them improve in these and other areas.

Remember, all kids need structure, love, and consistency; they need to be able to predict their environment. Your steadfast loving support along with consistent guidance and discipline will go a long way to creating the best environment for your kids. Give your children unconditional love and the opportunity to be the best they can be.

Alicia used to do psychological evaluations of students for a private day school, to determine if children were having learning and/or psychological difficulties. As a result, Alicia has a slightly different view of many of the labels we put on such children. She believes that some kids are labeled ADD or learning disabled simply because the way they learn doesn't match the teacher's style or even the prevailing style of instruction in the school system. Not everybody learns well in a classroom situation; some kids may just have too much energy to do well sitting five to six hours a day. Or a kid may process information differently than the way a teacher is delivering it. For the most part, the best thing we can do is to try to match the teaching to the child's learning style, not the other way around.

It's also possible that the child may be having trouble because he is picking up on the emotions of his classmates or his teacher. Intuitive children can sense these emotional currents and at times find it difficult to focus or to learn if the emotions are unsettling enough. Children with ADD or ADHD may be acting out negative emotions they are encountering in their environment. In such cases, teaching the child to put a white light of protection around him- or herself can be helpful; also, sending love to others can provide a barrier that will allow the child to maintain a strong emotional center. The best learning atmosphere you can give your child is one of love, acceptance, structure, and predictable discipline.

Parents and Children on the Other Side

Losing a child is one of the hardest things for anyone to endure, and one of my greatest privileges is helping grieving parents to reconnect with the spirits of children who have passed over. These children mostly want their parents to know they are well again and happy on the other side. They're usually fine—it's the ones who are left behind who need some kind of proof that these bright, young people are not gone forever, and that the love between parents and children still connects them at the deepest possible level.

Proof comes in many different ways. One mother had lost Chloe, her vivacious sixteen-year-old daughter, to an accidental drug overdose. I told her that her daughter had seen the mother take one of Chloe's stuffed animals and hold it while crying for hours. "Chloe's saying, 'Mama, please don't cry anymore,' " I told her. Then I picked up the movie character E.T. "She keeps saying, 'E.T., phone home'—what's that about?" I asked. The mother told me that Chloe had loved E.T. so much that they had placed a stuffed E.T. figure in the coffin with her. "Nobody knew that," she marveled.

Five days before Randi's ten-year-old daughter died, she asked her mom to get a reading from me. I was so touched and glad that I was able to tell Randi that her daughter was happy and peaceful and already working to help people from the other side. I also said that Randi would do the same kind of work here on earth by writing a book about her experiences. When I asked Randi why I kept being drawn to her neck, she pulled a locket out from under her blouse and told me it was inscribed with her daughter's name and birth date, and contained a lock of her daughter's hair. "She's always near my heart," Randi said with a smile. I felt happy that I was able to let her know that her daughter was still near and would be for all time.

Often the other children in a family will pick up intuitive messages from their deceased brothers or sisters. Unfortunately, they may not feel free to share them with their grieving parents or even be able to acknowledge these messages due to their own sadness. It breaks my heart to see these sad little souls, and I try to do everything I can to help them accept and be grateful for the communications they are receiving. For instance, a father and mother came on my TV show for a reading. They had lost their son James, who had been hyperactive and a handful, and both of them were feeling guilty because at times they had lost patience with him and gotten angry. James was able to tell them through me that he knew he was difficult at times but he couldn't help it, and he accepted his parents' apologies. Then I asked James's brother if he was sleeping in James's room now. "You feel his spirit come into the bedroom, don't you?" I asked. "Did James tell you, 'I'm happy, and tell Mother and Father that I'm happy'?" The little brother confirmed that he had had that exact experience and heard those exact words. This gave his father proof while it helped James's little brother to accept his intuitive side.

It turned out the healing wasn't just for James's family— his baby cousin Rose had passed over a few months earlier. I picked up the name Rose and the little girl's energy, and I was able to tell her parents (who were in the audience) that their daughter and James were playing together on the other side. I mentioned the special dress Rose had been buried in, and her father confirmed that a friend had made Rose a white dress embroidered with small red roses. I also told this couple that if they were thinking about having another child, they should go ahead—Rose wanted them to. The joy on the mother's face when she heard that made everyone's day.

This need for connection that goes beyond life and death is just as strong when parents pass over, and parents continue to watch over their children from the other side just as they do during their time on earth. To a brother and sister I passed along a message from their mother, Sara, that she truly appreciated the fact they were taking care of their father, and she wanted them to make sure they lived their own lives, too! Another time I picked a young girl out of a crowd at random and immediately sensed the spirit of Sam, her father. She started crying, and I looked over and saw two other girls crying as well. I said, "Oh my gosh, are those your sisters?" They all came over and I wanted to hug them—my arms weren't long enough to comfort them all. I was able to tell them that Sam was watching over them, to confirm that the dream the youngest girl had had was indeed a message from her dad, and that they should know Sam loved them and would always be with them in spirit. We all cried together, and it was a wonderful healing for three sweet, beautiful girls.

When I lost my own parents, it was incredibly painful—I still miss having their love and support on this earthly plane. And yet I feel my parents with me every day; I see them in my dreams and feel them near me. Parents and children share an eternal bond, one that we chose for ourselves long before we came into this life, and one that will exist far beyond death. This relationship can be nurtured with our inner wisdom, guided by our intuition, and most of all, shaped by our undying love for one another. Enjoy the gift of your children—they are young for such a short time, but they are your children forever.

9

Your Intuition on the Job

I've counted on my intuition for fifty years. I wouldn't be here if I didn't trust it. To me, intuition is paying careful attention to God's whispers.

—Quincy Jones

When I was growing up I didn't know that my life's work would be as a spiritual intuitive. As a teenager I loved music and theater and wanted to be a performer on Broadway. Then I got my college degree in secondary education and started substitute teaching. But I felt pulled to develop the psychic abilities that I'd had ever since I was a child. I followed that intuition and, with training and practice, I started to give readings to people. Now I travel all over the world giving readings, appearing on TV and radio, and teaching people to develop their sixth sense. So I guess in a way I'm still "performing" and teaching while fulfilling my destiny as a spiritual intuitive. Unbeknownst to me, the universe prepared me to be comfortable in front of an audience or a classroom.

I believe that even though some things are predestined we also have free will, and both free will and destiny show up in the choices we make about our careers. For example, many years ago I read for a woman and told her that her little boy, Mark, who was five years old at the time, would be a famous athlete in a solo kind of sport. He's now a skateboard champion.

Many of us have an innate sense of what our work should be in the world. We all have certain talents and abilities, and how (and whether) we use them is up to us. Sometimes, though, we get a little "push" from the other side. For instance, last year I was asked to do a workshop for a corporation on understanding energy and developing intuition. In the workshop a dark-skinned gentleman was sitting a little apart from most of the group. (Originally this man wasn't supposed to be at my workshop, but when he heard about it he felt called to be there and made special arrangements to be in the class.) I felt pulled to him, and in the middle of the workshop I walked over and asked if I could read for him.

I picked up on his grandfather Joseph right away. "Your grandfather's wearing some kind of hat on his head," I said. "It means something—is it a crown? Was your grandfather a king?" The gentleman confirmed his grandfather had indeed been the king of an African tribe. Joseph had some very specific directions about his grandson's career, but the information I was getting had nothing to do with Microsoft. Instead, it was all about politics. The man admitted he had an interest in pursuing a political career. "That will make your grandfather very happy," I said.

This man took my hand and looked sincerely into my eyes. "I cannot thank you enough," he said. "I've struggled with this for a long time. I feel pulled in two directions—the safe path of making money doing what I do now, and the more risky path of following my heart. I've been visualizing the answer coming to me for several months, and now it has through you." He gave me a warm hug.

Inner wisdom can help you recognize your talents and find ways to express them. It can also give you direction when it comes to:

- Choosing a career

- Getting a feel for the people at work

- Developing closer business relationships

- Avoiding potential pitfalls at your job

- Accessing greater creativity

- Performing your chosen work by connecting you to a source of awareness and information far beyond your own knowledge

But inner wisdom isn't just about being more successful in your profession, although it can help you to be so. Because you are partnering with universal energy and wisdom, using intuition in your career will help you learn more, do more, and create more than you could ever do on your own.

Sensing the Right Career or Job for You

Remember, logic, common sense, and intuition join to create wisdom and give you the most effective guidance in all areas of life, including your search for the best career or job. It begins by having a clear sense of your own talents and abilities. These may include everything from an aptitude with numbers, a flair for art or design, a capacity for working with your hands, a gift for writing, a propensity for organizing, or an inclination for taking care of people. What's your sense of the innate talents you have brought into this life?

Often these abilities show up when we're children. Maybe you were one of the kids who was always building something or taking something apart to figure out how it worked. Maybe you played doctor and took care of other kids when they got hurt. Maybe you drew pictures or made sculptures all the time. Maybe you were the one who always took the lead in playground games. What did you enjoy doing? Usually the things we enjoy are those that allow us to use our God-given gifts. If your parents, siblings, or childhood friends could describe you as a child, what would they say about you and the activities you enjoyed and at which you excelled? It's also possible that you have developed talents before this lifetime. I read recently that Tiger Woods hit his first golf ball at nine months, perfectly imitating his father's stance and stroke. How could a nine-month-old do such a thing? I believe that some child prodigies are accessing skills they learned in prior lives.

The other aspect of choosing a career or job in line with your inner wisdom is to find what makes you feel connected to something greater than yourself. I have found that the sense of a greater purpose is one clear signal from the universe that we are on our predestined career path. Author Norman Cousins wrote, "Each person has his or her own potential in terms of achievement and service. The awareness of that potential is the discovery of purpose; the fulfillment of that potential is the discovery of strength." When potential and purpose are guided by our inner wisdom, we experience our work as linked to the goals of a higher power. Our work not only allows us to express our talents and abilities but also makes a contribution to the world at large.

Once we have a clearer sense of the career path we feel is right for us, we can also use logic, common sense, and intuition to help us in the very mundane task of finding a job. Where should we look? Which positions should we apply for? Is this the right company? Should we take the job when it's offered? Is this the right position at the right pay? Intuition can help you sense the currents and hidden factors of every job you seek.

When we activate the law of attraction, we can start out with something simple. Asking to be led to the right opportunity or person opens us up to the many options that are all around us. You might "suddenly" notice a job posting at the coffee shop asking for a part-time salesperson, or a friend decides to start a band and asks you to join him. Perhaps you "accidentally" meet a literary agent at a party who gives you some great advice on getting your novel published at last. Your ability to visualize what you want, allow yourself to be led, and follow your intuition is the key to unlocking the new adventure.

Sometimes using your intuition can help you find the proper job in the first place. I was reading about a woman who had been out of work for some time and desperately needed a job. This woman was familiar with intuition and the practice of putting out an intention for what she wanted, so she had written a detailed description of her dream job. She also had been praying that she find work soon. That week she noticed a particular ad in the newspaper, describing a position that had nothing in common with her dream job description. Nonetheless, she felt called to send in a résumé. To her surprise she was called in for an interview. The interviewer told her that the position in the paper had been filled, but another position in the company had just opened up—one that perfectly matched the woman's dream job. She was hired immediately.

Another woman I read about received an offer for what appeared to be her dream job with a high-tech start-up company, but in this case she got a clear inner message not to take the position. Good thing, too, because three weeks later she heard the company had filed for bankruptcy.

Our inner wisdom always has our best interests at heart. If you allow it, it will help you make the best decisions that will bring you the lessons you need to learn and the success you are meant to achieve. However, you need to learn to listen to its directives very carefully and not to let your desires keep you from hearing the true inner voice. Sometimes we ask for inner guidance but all we want to hear is that the universe agrees with our desires. If the message is negative, we ignore it—even if we do so at our peril. Making a career decision may affect the course of your life for some time, so it's important to allow your intuition to speak clearly, keep your desires out of the way, and be willing to heed the messages you receive.

And remember, even if your choice ends up being wrong there may be a greater lesson for you in this particular job or career. In the United States, it's said that people will have an average of six or seven different *careers* (not jobs) over the course of their work lives. The key is to learn what you need from each step, and then move on (kind of like relationships!). And listen to your intuition even if it is prompting you to take chances, like starting your own business or trying a new profession. Don't allow yourself to be stuck or complacent or afraid to leave a secure job for the unknown. That's not what your inner wisdom wants for you. The voice inside is all about our fulfilling our full potential, which usually has to do with stretching, growing, being uncomfortable, and taking risks. Often the first indications that it's time to move on from a job or a career come from our inner wisdom—the still, small voice that whispers there's more to life than we're experiencing currently, and we have more that must be given or it will go to waste.

Many times common sense says keep your job until you find another. This may be a good idea, but don't be afraid to find another job. You'll have a "knowing" feeling when it's time to move on. Sometimes you may need to prepare to move on and be patient, waiting for the next opportunity to show up. Timing can be very tricky, but keep listening to your inner voice. Allow it to keep you growing and exploring new options, new outlets for your talents and abilities. If you neglect its promptings you may find the universe giving you a much larger kick in the rear, in the form of losing your job, getting sick, having your company go under, or even simply a feeling that you've died inside because you're no longer living your purpose. Your intuition will lead you places logic and common sense are not willing to go but that are in line with your place in the divine plan.

Intuition on the Job

There are many jobs where intuition actually comes in handy. In fact, in *most* jobs intuition comes in very handy. Intuition may tell a marketing director what ad campaign is going to be the best for a certain product. It may give an art expert a sense of discomfort, even nausea, when evaluating an artwork that turns out to be a fake. Intuition is absolutely essential in law enforcement and security work—anything where it's critical to sense dangerous situations and individuals before something happens. I've been around some extraordinary people who work as bodyguards for celebrities, and many of them have told me how much they rely on intuition to keep their clients safe.

But intuition shows up in many unlikely professions. For instance, I read about a professional fund-raiser who was contacting businesses for donations. He called a certain company and spoke with the owner, who pledged a certain amount. As soon as the fund-raiser hung up the phone he got an intuitive hit to call back and ask for more money (a real no-no in most cases). But he followed his intuition and called the same company immediately. The owner had just received an unexpected financial windfall, and he increased his original pledge amount.

We use intuition in many different ways on the job. Stockbrokers who review investment opportunities, venture capitalists who rate business plans, businesspeople who need to choose between different projects, technologies, personnel, and so on, all can use intuition as part of their evaluation process. They say things like, "This option *feels* better," or "I have a *sense* that this plan's going to work." Sometimes our intuitions are in alignment with logic and common sense, and sometimes they're not. Often our intuition can be used as the tiebreaker when one or more choices seem equally good.

Intuition also can point us in the direction of problems that aren't obvious. Safety experts can walk into a building and get a hit that there's a problem in a certain area. Computer experts and programmers may rely on instinct to lead them to the conflict that's making the system crash. Most of us in accomplishing the day-to-day tasks of our jobs often have a general sense when something's amiss. Intuitively we pick up on the small things that signal bigger problems, and then all of a sudden we make the connection and think, *I'd better check with marketing on this* or *Maybe finance should check these numbers again* or *I think this project might be sidelined,* or whatever our unconscious mind has discerned.

There are two other areas where intuition can help us be more successful on the job: in interpersonal relationships and as part of the decision-making process.

Intuition in Business Relationships

Think about all the different ways in which intuition can be helpful in business relationships. Great customer service people are able to get beyond the customer's emotions and discern what's really going on. Intuition also can help us sense what other people want. Salespeople are expert in using their intuition to find out what customers need and then presenting their product as the answer. They read the subtle cues of voice, body language, behavior, and also sense the energy and emotions of their clients. Based on these signs and signals, they can tell when the client is telling the truth and when the client may be exaggerating, when the objection is important or is something that doesn't need to be handled. They respond moment by moment to what they are sensing and lead the customers to the desired result: a sale.

In chapter 6 we talked about intuition in your personal relationships, but *every* relationship can benefit from your tapping into this key part of your inner wisdom. People are feeling creatures first, logical creatures second (or maybe ninth—most of us rely very little on logic when it comes to our relationships), and since very few of us express our feelings honestly and openly in business relationships, it makes sense to use our intuition to tune in to what other people are feeling. However, to do this, first you must make sure your own energy is clear and balanced. How much will you pick up if you're upset, angry, hungover, ill, or focused on something other than the situation at hand? What's worse, your own energy can affect the other person and you both end up feeling upset or angry. I hope that's never happened to you—but if it has, you know how painful it can be.

Give your inner wisdom a chance to be heard by clearing out your own energy first. If you're upset or agitated, calm your thoughts and emotions with a few deep breaths or a little meditation or a walk around the block. If you're not well physically, postpone your meeting—you're not going to make a good impression or give your best if your body is functioning at a lower level. And no matter what's happening, bring your focus to the person(s) with whom you will be meeting. Don't allow yourself to be preoccupied with past problems or future worries. The channel to your intuition is only tuned in when you are fully in the present moment so you can notice what you receive.

Now, suppose you're walking into a job interview or business meeting. You've never met the other person before or perhaps you've spoken with him on the phone, but this is your first face-to-face encounter. To prepare for your meeting intuitively, you might use a strategy described by Jack Canfield, the coauthor of the phenomenally successful *Chicken Soup for the Soul* series. Jack and his partner, Mark Victor Hansen, met with hundreds of small business owners to persuade them to sell *Chicken Soup for the Soul* in their establishments, and he suggests the following process for preparing for an important meeting. The night before, sit quietly and bring into your awareness the name and/or image of the person or people you'll be meeting with. Ask to know their fears, wants, and needs, and listen for the answers to come from your intuition. The next day you can walk into the meeting feeling completely prepared and connected, already tuned in to what the other people want and need. "We're all a little bit psychic," Jack says. "Most of us are not trained in that arena, but we don't have to be. We just have to ask the question."

When you arrive for the meeting, before you walk in the room, see what kind of intuitive hit you get. You may be able to sense the energetic currents that exist in the present moment, on your side as well as his. Have you ever gone to an appointment and just known things would go well? Conversely, have there been times when you know instinctively that the energy was slightly off? Pay attention to those intuitive indicators so you can adjust your energy and approach. Then as soon as you walk in the door, feel the other person's energy. This may immediately produce a lot of different thoughts and feelings that you may or may not understand. Pay attention to them, but don't try to filter them through logic. Those first moments before the logical, analytical part of the brain kicks in can provide some of the most valuable information for making the most of this meeting.

Use your intuition to help you adjust your approach to meet the other person where he is. For instance, maybe the other person feels nervous because you're better-looking or more accomplished. You could sit down quickly and put yourself at a lower level and talk in such a way that helps him feel more empowered and secure. Or if you're the one behind the desk, you may intimidate the other person. If that's not the energy you want to portray, come out from behind the desk and sit alongside the person on a couch or in a chair. It's also good to begin with small talk. This will give you a chance to feel out the other person intuitively while you seek commonalities. You'll have more of an opportunity to feel his energy so you can understand him.

Whenever we meet someone there is a constant, nonverbal communication of energy going on that either strengthens or weakens what we say. When we tune in to that current of energy we stand a much better chance of communicating in such a way that the other person will want to help us. When we're really attuned, a meeting can become like a dance with a compatible partner. We somehow know what subject to bring up and when, we feel confident, and our words flow smoothly. Our goals become the goals of the other person and vice versa.

Remember, though, your own energy needs to be balanced and clear; otherwise you can end up resonating negatively with the other person. Imagine someone who's very insecure walking into a business meeting with an equally insecure individual. Either the two of them will have enormous rapport with each other, or the insecurity will build up until both of them become paranoid. (Don't laugh, I've seen it happen.) But if you walk in with balanced energy, feeling grounded and ready to be your best, then if you sense insecurity or anger or upset it's not going to push your buttons. Instead of being affected by negativity you can actually help the other person get into a better place. When you're grounded and balanced, sometimes all it takes is a kind word or asking, "Are you okay? Did you have a good day?" to change the energy of someone else. Sometimes taking a moment to be kind can make all the difference.

Intuition also can help protect you from those who don't necessarily have your best interests at heart. Unfortunately, some people take the dog-eat-dog side of business very seriously and believe that they have to step on others so that they themselves may advance. Intuition can help you sense other people's hidden agendas and keep you tuned in to unspoken politics in the office. You can keep the negative energy of others away from you in the workplace by taking a few minutes before you arrive to put a white light of protection around yourself. And don't buy into their negativity; you don't need to contribute even more bad energy to an unhealthy situation. Keep your own energy positive and as healthy as possible. If things get really bad, leave. You don't want to subject yourself to prolonged negative energy if you have any choice in the matter.

Happily, many of the relationships we develop on the job are some of the best and the strongest we have. We share experiences, goals, successes, and failures with our work colleagues; we know about their families and the high and low points in their lives. We bring so much to our jobs, it's not surprising that we can "leave" a certain energy when we depart. You may have had the experience of feeling a psychic residue from the previous jobholder when you moved into a new position. It could be the attitude colleagues have toward the person in that job or to the circumstances that caused the position to be open.

In one recent case, the psychic residue was attributable to the spirit of a woman who had recently died. At an intuition workshop I gave for the staff of a magazine, a woman stood up and said, "A colleague of ours died giving birth to her second child a few weeks ago. We'd like to know if you could pick up on her." I had mentioned this woman's initials in a couple of the short readings I had given earlier, but once the question was asked she came through very strongly. I walked over to a girl in the audience and asked her if she had a particular connection with the woman who had passed over. "Do you have Karen's job now? You're sitting at her desk, aren't you?" I asked. She nodded. "And did you send a letter to her parents?" "Yes, but nobody knew that," she answered. "You still have Karen's picture on your desk, don't you?" I asked. Then I passed along messages for Karen's husband and children and added that their coworker had been really touched by the way so many of them had come together at the office to say goodbye to her. "Did something happen with the electricity today in your building?" I asked. "Yes, the lights were blinking on and off." "That was Karen; she wants you all to know that her energy is still here."

Every relationship we have, whether on the job or in the rest of our lives, as long as there is shared love and affection, creates a bond that can exist beyond our leaving the position or leaving this earth. That's why it's so important to cherish our relationships and do our best to make the most of them for ourselves and our friends, colleagues, and loved ones.

Decision Making and Intuition

The other place in business where intuition is essential is somewhat surprising, given intuition's "fluffy" reputation. But more and more organizations—from the U.S. Marines and the army to firefighters to corporate experts and executives from all sorts of industries—are recognizing the vital contribution of intuition to decision making. In a 1982 study of intuition reported in a psychology journal, several businesspeople were classified as very intuitive or less intuitive based on their ability to guess playing cards. The group was then asked to make decisions on a series of managerial problems. The very intuitive businesspeople were evaluated as making "significantly better decisions" than the less intuitive group.

Studies have shown that the more senior the manager in a company, the more he or she is inclined to rely on intuitive decision making. A 1984 study reported in the *Harvard Business Review* lists five ways senior managers use intuition in business:

- To sense when a problem exists

- To help them focus on what's really important in familiar situations

- To integrate data and experience into the context of the big picture; to evaluate rational analysis from another perspective

- To move past analysis and reach solutions quickly

According to Gary Klein, author of *The Power of Intuition: How to Use Your Gut Feelings to Make Better Decisions at Work,* today's rapidly changing business world requires enhanced speed, flexibility, and adaptability—"precisely the kinds of qualities that can be enhanced by intuitive decision making." Klein studied experienced firefighters to determine how some of them could sense where a fire would move, while novices could not accomplish the same task. The firefighters had absorbed so much experience with different kinds of fires and burning buildings that their knowledge was now stored on the subconscious rather than the conscious level. When these firefighters encountered a fire, their subconscious compared it with all the other fires they had seen and gave a lightning-fast assessment of what the fire would do next. However, I believe intuition not only connects us to our subconscious references but also to sources of information and wisdom that extend far beyond our own experience. When we draw upon intuition to help us make decisions, we can sense patterns and currents of energy that we cannot see or know about consciously.

Of course, intuition isn't the only factor you want to use when making decisions. Analysis—what I call logic and common sense—also needs to be applied to make the best decisions possible. Analyzing numbers, assessing the pros and cons of the situation, and doing projections and business plans are all extremely important. However, as Herbert Simon, an expert on decision making who won the 1978 Nobel Prize in economics, asserts, important decisions can't be made through analysis alone because there are just too many factors to take into account. The more complex the decision, the more factors there are and the harder it is to analyze them.

What's more, as business scandals in the United States and elsewhere have shown, numbers and projections can be made to lie. Intuition can be a very important gut check to tell us when some data or a financial report seems too good to be true, or when the individual who provides the analysis might be fudging the numbers to make the company, the department, or the person look good. When it comes to any decisions having to do with people, analysis will take you only so far, and intuition—which is better at picking up the human factor—must be taken into account.

Earlier I suggested using logic, common sense, and intuition as your three means of evaluating and making any choice. In terms of business, the same three factors apply. When making a decision, always start with your intuition. What hit do you get immediately? Make note of your initial response to a problem or situation, as this response may contain information inaccessible to your conscious mind. Even when setting business goals, ask yourself, "Is this goal right for me at this time?" It could be that pretesting your goals helps you hear the faint voice in your head that says, "Yes, but with the new baby on the way . . ." or "I'd really prefer to spend more time doing the work itself instead of managing a larger staff." Before you invoke the law of attraction, it's helpful to know if what you are trying to attract is what you really want.

Second, review the problem logically. Make a list of the factors involved in the decision and gather any information you may need to understand the situation more fully. List the pros and cons of the different resolutions to the situation. (Using logic helps you to separate yourself from the situation and keeps your desires and emotions out of the way for a while. While emotions are a valid factor to consider in your decision, you need to evaluate using cold, clear logic to get a fresh perspective.) Come up with different scenarios based on your logical analysis, and see if any of them are in line with your first intuitive response.

Third, apply your common sense. Take a look at your own emotions, beliefs, prejudices, and so on, and make sure they are not influencing you too much. Play out different scenarios in your mind and see what the consequences of each will be. Is this decision practical? What things haven't you taken into account? Could anything go wrong? If so, can you fix it, and if not, will you be comfortable with the consequences? If you're still uncertain, you may want to consult with other people; in some circumstances an outside perspective makes good sense.

Finally, do a gut check on the choice you want to make. Sometimes the most logical choice still isn't the right one— there are human factors that common sense and logic haven't given enough weight to, or perhaps there's something coming down the road that you may not yet know consciously but your intuition is warning you about. If you feel you're too close to the situation, you can sometimes ask friends for their opinion. By talking about it, their ideas can help open your eyes and put the decision into perspective. Talking with someone who cares can help you understand what's being given to you in guidance. Give your intuition the chance to have a final vote on your decision, and let it continue to weigh in every step of the way as the decision unfolds. You'll find your inner wisdom may give you a greater ability to pick up on and adapt to changes, far more than the plodding "analysis paralysis" approach.

Accessing Your Creative Energy

Where does creativity come from? How do artists produce something from nothing? How do scientists and inventors pull new theories, technological advances, or scientific breakthroughs out of thin air? What is the source of genius? Creativity and inspiration are born not of the conscious mind but within the realm of intuition. Diogenes' cry of "Eureka!" when he understood why water sloshed out of his bathing pool; Leonardo da Vinci's concept of a helicopter five hundred years before one could be built; Michelangelo's depiction of the Last Judgment in the Sistine Chapel; Mozart's symphonies; Edison's phonograph; Einstein's theory of relativity; and Picasso's paintings reach far beyond the experience of the individual and bring into form the energy of the divine. I teach people that intuition is a creative process because it connects us to wisdom and energy that is beyond ourselves as we tap into the universal source of all creation.

Almost every artist will tell you she has no clue where her creative energy comes from, and prominent scientists such as Jonas Salk and Albert Einstein also have acknowledged the role intuition can play in discoveries and breakthroughs. Intuition allows us to make connections between seemingly unrelated ideas and references, and to access information that we have not encountered directly ourselves. When most scientists and artists describe creativity, they talk about a feeling that energy is flowing through them, not from them, that their inspiration comes from somewhere far beyond their own experience. It's almost as if they are channeling the art or science or thought that is being given to them from a more universal plane.

How can you tap into your own creativity? First, you might quiet your mind. In that space, ask to be given creative insight, and then listen. Creativity can show up in many different ways, but often the conscious mind's chatter can mask the "still, small voice" of the creative impulse. Many creative people make a conscious commitment to finding time to listen to their inner voice. I read of one high-powered businesswoman who regularly took time away from the office to listen to her inner creative impulse. On one such creative "vacation" she came up with a new strategy that increased the value of her company by several million dollars.

Second, start to recognize the creative impulse when it arrives. There are probably as many ways to feel the creative urge as there are to feel an intuitive hit. For you, it could be a sense of rightness, of everything aligning in the moment; or perhaps it feels like a whirlwind of energy in which new possibilities emerge constantly. It could be a sure knowing, or an excitement, or a rush of pleasure. It even could be somewhat painful, like the birth of a baby—you struggle and push until the new idea or vision emerges full-blown and beautiful. However your creative impulse signals its presence, learn to recognize the signs so you can do your best to keep the flow of energy going.

Once you recognize your creative/intuitive impulse, you can learn to ride its energy like a surfer rides a wave. This energy of "flow," similar to that experienced by athletes who are operating at their peak, makes us feel as if we are connected to something other than ourselves, a greater source of inspiration and possibility than we can access through our conscious mind. I believe it's an energy similar to that which I experience when I give readings—tapping into a power larger than my own consciousness and experience, the power that makes the universe run and flowers bloom and the stars revolve in the heavens.

Once you're on the creative "wave," so to speak, take advantage of it. Capture whatever your creative impulse is bringing into your consciousness. Write it down, speak it, draw it, design it, make it—use the form your creativity demands. And recognize that creativity has its own rise and fall. Creativity and intuition are never one sided; they are your connection to the greater energy of the universe, and that connection is not something that necessarily works on demand. If it's not coming, don't worry; it will come in its own time. Do what you can to increase your access to creativity and intuition and then give thanks for it when it arrives, recognizing it as a gift from the universe.

Creating the Energy of Success

There is an energy of success that we all can feel. It's the sensation that things are on an upward spiral, that the universe is collaborating with you in bringing this situation or venture to a happy conclusion. Part of business and career intuition is becoming more sensitive to the earliest stirrings of the energy of success and following its directions as much as possible. This is not to say you don't have to work to keep the energy of success flowing! I've worked hard through the years sharing my gift through readings and in the media. I believe I've been partnering with the energy of the universe to let people know how to access and use their inner wisdom, and the universe has helped by directing me to opportunities to expand

and grow. On my part, I've done my best to take the opportunities that have presented themselves. I believe opportunity provided by the universe, augmented by your preparedness and willingness to work, equals success. When you tap into your inner wisdom and allow it to guide you, it will bring you what you need in the time you need it. Your job is to seize the opportunities and partner with the universe in your own success.

Sad to say, sometimes we get so caught up in our own story and circumstances that we actually block the manifestation of success the universe might be sending our way. I had a client recently, a woman who's both an actress and a screenwriter. Throughout her reading she was obsessing about success and worrying about every possible audition, phone call, interview, and so on. Her negative energy was literally blocking any possibility of her tuning in to the opportunities that might have come to her. I finally told her, "I understand that you're frustrated, but you're so desperate that you're putting out that energy everywhere, and people don't like it. You're blocking the energy of success and you're not doing anything to fix it. There's no way you will be successful unless you start working on your anxieties and negativity first. If you keep on doing what you're doing, you're going to create the very destiny you don't want."

People have to break the habit of negative energy for good things to flow to them. The antidotes to negative energy are hope and faith. You have to have faith that things happen in time, that it's the journey that matters, and what comes your way will teach you the lessons you were meant to learn—like faith and persistence. The key is to enjoy the ride no matter how it is or what it is or what's going on, and keep working to stay in tune with the energy of the universe. Trust that the right things will unfold in your life at the right time. As human beings our tendency is to want what we want *right now*! But the universe's timeline may be different. Take Leonardo DiCaprio—he first bought the rights to the story of Howard Hughes several years before he could get the movie studios to agree to make the film. But when he bought the rights he was far too young to even think of playing the character of Howard Hughes. Because the universe delayed the project, DiCaprio played Hughes in *The Aviator* and was nominated for an Academy Award.

Our goal in life is to fulfill our potential, and in that is our success. We can create success through our own efforts, but it's a hard, uphill slog. But when we partner with the universe, our journey to success can be much easier. Using our inner wisdom to connect with the universal currents of energy, seizing the opportunities presented to us, trusting in the universal timing while putting forth positive energy and effort, and learning the lessons we are meant to learn as we pursue our goals will help us attain a success that will far exceed money, fame, and power—because our success will be in alignment with our own highest good and greatest growth. We will become what we are capable of becoming, and in that we can rejoice.

10

Dollars and Your Uncommon Sense

Inside the energy of abundance, there is no struggle, only flow.
—Stuart Wilde, *The Trick to Money Is Having Some*

Do you know someone who just has a "feel" for money? A person who seems to pick the right investments intuitively? Someone who goes to Las Vegas and comes home a winner every time? (My dad used to do very well at the track, and I have a good friend who always wins when he gambles.) Don't those people drive you crazy?

For most of us money and finances are sources of a lot of confusion and even more stress. We obsess about our bank balance or avoid balancing our checkbooks because we just don't want to know how much money we have. We worry about our retirement savings—especially those of us who were heavily invested in the U.S. stock market in the year 2000 and saw our 401(k)s become 201(b)s! When offered an investment opportunity, we either:

- Turn it down right off the bat because we don't like it or understand it

- Accept it willy-nilly without evaluating it intuitively or otherwise

- Analyze it thoroughly, weighing all the pros and cons, reading up on the kind of investment if we're not familiar with it, consulting other experts to make sure it's a solid choice, and end up suffering from "analysis paralysis"

- Get an intuitive hit on the investment and rush into it based solely on that

I think any of those four choices is not the best way to invest or manage our money. From everything I've seen, heard, and read, the most successful investors and financiers use a combination of left-brain analysis and right-brain intuition. David Silverman, director of the Chicago Mercantile Exchange in the 1990s, once wrote "All great traders know that attaining profitability is not simply a mechanical endeavor but a creative, intuitive process." At the same time, we read books on manifesting our dreams of easily-gotten wealth. It's normal. It's human. And it's also possible—if you attune yourself to your "money intuition."

Occasionally I tune in to information for my clients about money, contracts, business dealings, investments, and so on. Years ago I told one client to invest in a thing called "e-mail."

I didn't know what it was at the time, but I knew it would be hot. However, I'm terrible at gambling; I can go to Las Vegas and lose money more often than not. (Once in a while I will get a hit about something—mostly when to leave the black-jack table. I never make more than about sixty dollars but it keeps me from losing.) I can't pick up the business section of the newspaper and get a hit on the next big stock. Making massive amounts of money by using my intuition is not why I was given my abilities. However, I do check out all my own investments intuitively. For years I also worked with a broker who was intuitive. She's retired now, but in the last ten years we both felt that gold would do well, and it did, and oil would do well, and it did. This broker would suggest things to me and if they felt right, I would go for it. I often pick up on oth-ers' financial opportunities. I can feel if a business venture, contract, or deal is a good one or not.

For example, in a reading for a very successful songwriter, politician, and radio DJ, I warned him that he might need to iron out details for a new project he was undertaking, and I suggested he have an attorney look over everything; I felt there was a great possibility for success but he needed to check everything carefully and stay strong in the negotiations, con-firming his feeling about this as well. (Frequently in readings I'm confirming people's instincts.) I also picked up on a piece of property he owned near the water. He said he was thinking of building a house on the land, and again, I felt it would be a good investment for him. (This gentleman was very skeptical about intuition until I told him I was seeing a new car for him. Very surprised, he said he had been driving the same car for sixteen years and he really loved it. But it had been giving him problems recently and that very day he had decided to get rid of it and get a new car. I think that convinced him about my abilities more than anything else I could have said!)

You can use intuition to pick up on all kinds of information about what you should do with your money, where you should invest, what you should buy, where you should be careful, and where you can take calculated risks. I have known many people who had the ability to pick up on the energy that money puts out, to tune in to it, and to do very well financially as a result. And while I *always* tell people to use logic and common sense as well as intuition when they make financial decisions, I believe that we can learn to use our inner wisdom to make better decisions about finances, investments, financial advisors, and every other aspect of the monetary side of life.

Using Intuition, Logic, and Common Sense to Help You with Money

Money is actually a representation of the exchange of energy. Joseph Campbell once said, "Money is congealed energy, and releasing it releases life's possibilities." When you look at money this way, it becomes very clear that we should be able to tune in to the energy of money in the same way we tune in to our own energy with health or the energy of others in relationships. Some people are very good with money energy; to put it another way, they "speak money." And it's very interesting to hear how most of these financial adepts view their moneymaking abilities. Yes, they may be investing and/or financial experts; and in some cases they've spent a lot of time learning about their particular area. But at a certain point almost all of them admit that they get a sense of whether something is going to make them money or not. Their decision making goes beyond the analytical, conscious side and taps into something much deeper. It's at this point that both intuition and inner wisdom come into play.

For instance, the husband of one of my students somehow always ended up on the right side of any business or financial transaction. He bought a house in what was considered a bad part of town, and everyone told him he'd never make his money back on the investment. Well, he sold the house a year later for a twenty-five-thousand-dollar profit. My friend Gary Hughes is also pretty good. Whenever he works on a business deal he takes a moment to listen to his gut feeling before he ever consults his logical side. "If my gut says no, I pay attention," he says. He's made a lot of money by paying attention to his intuitive side. These are the kind of people you want to study when it comes to tapping into your own inner money wisdom.

However, intuition is only one-third of the inner wisdom you must apply to your finances. In the same way it's absolutely vital to apply logic, common sense, and intuition when it comes to your health, it's even more essential to listen to all three when it comes to your money. After all, your intuition would probably not be very good at balancing your checkbook! But it can be an important source of information whenever you're evaluating a possible business deal, investment property, stock tip, financial professional, and so on.

Suppose you have a good friend who brings you an investment opportunity. He is involved in a start-up business, and he's asking you to invest ten thousand dollars in exchange for a certain number of stock options when the company goes

Discover Your Inner Wisdom ✦ 185

public in about a year. The logic part of your inner wisdom asks to see the company's financials and its business plan. It also prompts you to do some research into the industry and the company itself. Common sense tells you to get everything in writing. It also tells you to visit the company if at all possible, to check out the people and the atmosphere. Common sense also may tell you that if you are not an experienced investor, you should have your accountant or another financial professional review everything before you put your money on the table!

Let's say you've done all your research and you've checked everything out to the best of your ability. You've employed your logic and common sense and all indications are that this would be a good investment. Now you bring your intuition into play. Using the method described in chapter 3, you get quiet and ask yourself the question, "Is this a good investment for me at this time?" All of a sudden you start to get a queasy feeling in your stomach, or perhaps you hear a voice in your head saying "Stay away!" Or maybe you're driving down the road and all you notice are stop signs and billboards with slogans like "Save your money for a rainy day" or "Hold on to your hard-earned cash." For whatever reason, your intuition is telling you not to make the investment. You turn down your friend, thanking him for the opportunity. He shakes his head and tells you you're making a mistake, but you stick to your guns.

Then, a month later, your child is hospitalized with a serious illness. The medical bills are mounting up and the ten thousand dollars you were thinking of investing is used to pay the hospital. Or perhaps a few months down the road your friend comes to you and says there's been a problem with the company's main product, and they are indefinitely postponing taking the company public. All you can think is, *Thank goodness my intuition protected me!*

When you combine intuition with logic and common sense, you're tapping into a source of information and guidance that you cannot get any other way. You're looking beyond the obvious and sensing the currents of energy and wisdom that are flowing around and through us at all times—currents that also control the flow of the energy of money into our lives. Using all your inner wisdom can help you attract more of the energy of money to you while helping you stay clear of possible financial problems and potential loss.

Becoming a Money Magnet

Recently I read a story about a woman who sorely needed money. One night she dreamed that she had the winning lottery numbers for the Megabucks game in the adjoining state. She woke up and decided to drive one hundred miles into the next state to purchase lottery tickets. But on the way there she got cold feet, and instead of playing all five of the numbers in her dream, she played three of the dream numbers and two others. Well, all five of the numbers in her dream were picked. The jackpot, which was split between three people, amounted to around $2.5 million. Her three numbers were worth nothing.

I believe each of us has the potential to become a money magnet, but we have to do the things that will attract money to us and make sure we get rid of any inner barriers to having money in our lives. This woman did something to bring the winning lottery numbers into her mind: maybe it was the intensity of her desire, or perhaps it was her reasons for wanting the money. On the other hand, for her to dream all five winning numbers and play only three indicates to me that either she didn't trust her inner wisdom or she had some barrier inside that was preventing her from accepting her good fortune.

If money is basically energy, then we should be able to attract that energy and help it to manifest. I believe that intuition is one of the most effective gateways to manifesting anything we want in life. Intuition taps into the knowledge of the universe to reveal to us what is unseen, and manifestation taps into the power of the universe to bring the unseen into physical form. In manifestation, we put our wishes, will, intention, and intuitive wisdom to work for us to bring our desires to fruition.

My life is full of examples of the power of manifestation. For many years I have had what I call a "wish board"—a bulletin board on which I post words and pictures cut out of magazines that represent what I want to accomplish and who I want to draw into my life. My friend Chantal told me about wish boards, and it's been a godsend in my life. In almost every case, as soon as I put something on my wish board—getting a new book contract, for instance, or appearing on a particular TV show—and I focus on that goal, within six months to a year it comes true. A wish board is just one form of manifestation; you can do the same thing simply by focusing your intent and desire on a goal. You have the power to will what you want into being anytime you tap into your inner wisdom and allow the universe to help and guide you.

There are many ways we can manifest being a money magnet. Believing that abundance is our natural state is a

188 ♦ Char Margolis

great place to start. Universal energy is unlimited, and we can tap into that energy and bring ourselves as much or as little as we want. The question is always, just how much are we willing to accept? There's a great parable about going to the ocean and dipping water out of its vastness. The ocean doesn't care whether we use a teaspoon, a coffee cup, a bucket, or a hundred-gallon tanker truck. Its job is simply to be the ocean, and to provide for us all the abundance we could ever want. When we start by believing that abundance is everywhere, and we only have to bring the tanker truck to the ocean instead of a teaspoon to have everything we want, it sets up an energetic field that will help us attract money into our environment.

We talked earlier about the power of intention, and it's vitally important to be very clear on your intentions around money so you can put the force of your desire behind them. What do you want money for? Do you want money so you'll always be secure? Do you want to take care of your children or your parents? Do you want to become more powerful or influential or successful and you think money will make you so? Do you want money to travel, to learn, to grow, to contribute to others, to make a difference in the world? Do you want money so you can have fun? What will having money mean to you and to the other people in your life? Once you know what you want money for, you can set intentions that are driven by your deepest desires.

Now, check your intentions with your intuition. This means that you need to get quiet and listen to the inner voice or the sense of rightness inside. Is this particular wish for money in line with your highest good? If it is, then you stand a good chance of being able to tap into the energy of money.

Getting clear about our money intentions also requires that we take a look at our attitudes about money and identify anything that may be holding us back. Like the woman who dreamed the winning lottery numbers, we don't want to turn our backs on the abundance the universe is offering us! If money is energy and abundance is the natural state of the universe, it follows that whenever we experience lack, problems with money, or obstacles in our path, we need to do a gut check to see if we are getting in our own way. Remember that old expression "Money is the root of all evil"? If you believe that, do you think you'll attract money easily? (By the way, the real quote, from the Bible, is "The love of money is the root of all evil," which to me means that loving money for its own sake can pull us away from valuing what's truly important—our love for one another and our connection with universal spirit.) Most of us have some funky ways of looking at money that keep us from accepting full abundance in our lives. Some people grew up poor and ended up hating the rich or believing that all rich people got their money by being dishonest. Others grew up wealthy and never valued the abundance they had; they didn't take care of the riches entrusted to them and instead wasted their money's energy. Still others believe money can get in the way of entering the Kingdom of Heaven, as in the parable of the camel going through the needle's eye. Other people have had bad experiences with their own finances—problems with taxes, arguments over money that split families, and so on—that cause them to associate only negative emotions with wanting or pursuing money. Any or all of these beliefs or incidents are not necessarily important, *except* when you want to become a money magnet.

To draw the energy of money to you, to become the conduit of greater abundance, you must make sure your "money channel" is cleared of any psychic or psychological debris that might impede the flow. Start by examining your own past history with money and abundance. Is there anything that stands out as a negative experience or belief about finances or the role of money in life? Once you're aware of anything, work on it. Go see a counselor. Do whatever it takes to get past any fears you have about having money. Get one of the many excellent self-help books out there that teach you how to get rid of old beliefs or to resolve negative experiences from your past. Once you've gotten rid of the old "junk," decide how you want to view money and abundance from now on. Maybe you need to believe that God wants you to live an abundant life. Maybe you need to focus not on what money will give you but on the good you will do when you have greater abundance. You have to find the balance between the material and the spiritual world. Remember, money will give you choices, and you can always choose to spend it on healing and helping yourself and others.

You also need to take care of two things in your psychological makeup before you're ready to be a money magnet. The first is fear. Fear is the one emotion that will stifle intuition and impede the flow of any energy from the universe, including abundance. Fear shuts us down; it keeps us from seeing the opportunities that come our way and taking the opportunities we do notice. If you're afraid of the responsibility that more money will bring; if you're worried that you'll be a different person if you have more money; if you're concerned that having to earn more money will give you less time with your family or make you less spiritual, then you'll sabotage any chance you have to attract greater abundance into your life.

Do whatever it takes to get past any fears you have about money. Would the universe give you wealth if it was going to result in your ultimate harm? Check your inner wisdom again to discover the truth that will release you from these unfounded fears. You are bigger than any of your fears; your connection to spirit and your guidance from universal love can keep you on the right path even if you do have more abundance. When you keep your channel of inner wisdom clear, you will be able to take care of the greater levels of abundance that you will attract once your fear is out of the way.

The second thing you must handle is the tendency to play small—to approach the ocean of abundance with a teaspoon thinking that that's all you want or deserve. Opening yourself to greater abundance is a service to both yourself and human-kind. I agree with Nelson Mandela, who told the people of South Africa in his inaugural address that it is our responsibil-ity to manifest the glory of God that is in each of us. We serve the world best by claiming our greatness and accepting the abundance God offers to us when we do our best.

When our intentions are in line with our inner wisdom, when we feel that what we desire will be in line with our high-est good, when we banish fear and eliminate any old psycho-logical garbage that we've accumulated about money, when we accept our calling to fill ourselves with the abundance that surrounds us, then we are ready to put the force of our emo-tions and desires behind our intentions and send them out into the universe. We're ready to offer our full, joyous, com-mitted attention to seizing the opportunities that show up and creating more abundance in our lives. *In*tention, combined with *attention*, combined with strong, positive emotion, is like a laser beam signaling "I'm ready! Start the money stream coming now!"

Intuitive Investing: Is This a Good Investment?

Several years ago a gentleman came to me to ask about selling his business. Should he accept the offer from an investment group to buy him out with payments over time? My hit on the situation was to sell for cash immediately. The man took less money for an all-cash deal, and within two years the group went out of business. If the man had agreed to the proposed payment plan, he never would have gotten his money.

Most of us have heard stories where a deal that looks good on paper just "feels" wrong or too good to be true. If this happened to you, I hope you were smart enough to follow your intuitive caution and stay away. But of course, there are far too many people who ignore such warnings. As financial advisor Suze Orman writes, "There are many ways the universe offers us guidance to protect ourselves, but we usually just turn our backs on this guidance." Unfortunately, those who turn their backs usually pay the price, literally, for their psychic blindness.

Intuition should always play a part in our investment decisions. Intuition can help us evaluate not only the people who bring us the investments but also the investment itself. We can get a hit on whether this person is honest or good for us or tapped into the universal energy of money. We also can get a sense of whether this investment opportunity feels like it's right for us. I'm not suggesting that you only use intuition to guide your investment choices. That's like trying to catch a fish with a pole but no line or hook. As I said before, you need all three components of inner wisdom—logic, common sense, and intuition—to make your best choices when it comes to investing your money well.

One of the key decisions you will make about your money is choosing the right financial advisor, and your inner wisdom absolutely should play a part in the decision-making process. Say that you need to choose a financial advisor to help you create a college fund for your children and invest for retirement. You start with logic: find advisors who understand the kinds of investing you wish to do. In the United States, financial companies often have specialists in educational investing, retirement investing, and so on. If you think you want mostly stocks and bonds, you'd go to one kind of advisor; if you want bank investments or insurance, you'd go to another. That's logic.

Common sense might tell you to ask your friends if they have investment goals that are similar to yours. If so, what advisors do they have and what kinds of results have they gotten? Common sense might also tell you to approach friends who are on the same socioeconomic level as you, or perhaps a little higher. If you only have thousands of dollars to invest, it doesn't make sense to ask for a referral to a financial advisor who only sees clients with a net worth in the millions. Once you have the referrals, common sense might tell you to call these advisors, talk to them about your general situation and see what they say, and then set up meetings with one or two.

But how do you know which advisor will be the best for you? You can listen to their information using all of your logic and common sense, but if you're really smart, you'll let your intuition have a say in the final choice. Your intuition will allow you to tune in to things that are unspoken and unseen. Especially in the current environment, where hidden fees and costs seem to be a part of every investment and honesty and a fair rate of return seem to take a backseat to overstated marketing claims and "get rich quick" schemes, sometimes the only way you can get past the hype is by using your sixth sense. Intuitively checking the financial advisor, the investment vehicle, and the deal in general can save you a lot of money and heartache that might not be prevented with logic and common sense alone.

But letting your intuition be the only thing you consult would be as stupid as relying solely on logic and common sense. Say you intuitively feel really good about one of your financial advisor candidates. He or she just seems to be a great fit for you and your financial needs. That's great—but you still need to check the person out using your conscious, logical mind. She could feel right because she has come into your life to teach you a great lesson, maybe about trusting people too easily. Or maybe he's supposed to be part of your life in a way other than financially—as a good friend, or a potential business partner, or even a romantic relationship. That good feeling also could come from a past life connection between you. In the same way you check logic and common sense with intuition, you must let logic and common sense have input once your intuition has had its say. You'll know how good your investment advisors are by the results they help you produce.

I believe that most investment decisions must start with logic and common sense. Invest only in things that you understand and that make sense given your investment goals. Learn about what you are putting your money into, and keep up with overall economic trends. Pay attention to your invest-ments; don't rely on anyone else to care about your money the way you do. (Professional investor Marcus Goodwin comments that when it comes to investing, most of us feel more comfortable listening to the advice of people we don't know, who might not have our best interests at heart, and who might not have the expertise they claim, rather than listening to our own inner voice and allowing it to have input in our financial decisions!) Follow the basic rules of sound investing, including asset allocation. And finally, give your intuition and your gut feeling a vote when it comes to your investment de-cisions. Check out your gut feelings about your financial ad-visors and the investment vehicles they choose. If something feels wrong, don't do it. Even if you miss out on a big profit, there will be another opportunity.

If something feels right, go ahead and put money into it, af-ter you've done your research. Every once in a while, intuition will give you a hit and you have to go with it. Pay attention to the clues the universe may be offering you through your intu-ition, coincidences, dreams, and so on. I once read a story of a Wall Street investor who had a dream as a child of eight or so in the 1960s. He dreamt of Abraham Lincoln (of all people), who told him, "Technology awaits, follow Bill through the gates." Fifteen years later this little boy became a stockbroker and heard about a company called Microsoft, founded by Bill Gates. He got in on the stock early and made millions.

When you're investing in the stock market, you also have to know when to pull out. Again, logic and common sense may tell you when it's time to sell, but your gut also may signal you long before logic and common sense weigh in. George Soros, the billionaire investor, gets a pain in his back that tells him it's time to sell a position. Rely on every pillar of your inner wisdom to help you make money and prevent losses.

The Gifts of Universal Abundance

I don't think it's an accident that the U.S. one-dollar bill has all kinds of mystical and spiritual symbols on it—pyramids and the all-seeing eye of God, to name two. Money symbolizes one of the great principles of the universe: abundance. But it's only one part of the abundance that can fill our lives if we open ourselves to it and endeavor to make our inner selves reflect the abundance we wish to attract.

I believe there are four simple ways to connect to all of the divine abundance that is our birthright. First, take care of what you already have. The universe wants to be certain that we will be worthy stewards for the treasure it is ready to pour into our laps. If we don't take the time to balance our checkbooks, if we ignore calls from our brokers or banks, if we spend money we don't have on things we don't need, we are not being responsible with our current wealth. To be ready for abundance, clean up your financial act; it's like cleaning your house before an important guest comes to stay.

Second, signal your willingness to receive. I read about a man who picks up pennies wherever he sees them, even in muddy gutters. A penny doesn't buy anything these days, but he believes that it's his responsibility to accept all money that comes his way no matter how insignificant. Being ready to receive might mean learning more about finances; it might mean opening a savings account or an investment account with a brokerage, or going to see a financial planner. It definitely means getting rid of any mental and emotional blocks to abundance, as described earlier in this chapter. I know some people who swear by creating lists of financial goals, or making a commitment to support a certain charity, or creating "treasure maps" with images of what their increased abundance will allow them to do, have, or be.

Third, give to others. Giving tells the universe that we are part of the great cycle of abundance. Giving to others also will make you feel more abundant. I have a friend who makes a point of always giving something to everyone who asks her. Even if she's approached by five panhandlers in a row, she will give each of them at least a dollar. She believes so strongly in her rule that I've seen her give a guy a twenty-dollar bill because it was the only thing she had in her wallet. Sharing your wealth with another, even if you share the smallest amount, can open you up to receive even more in your life.

Fourth, be grateful no matter what. Every spiritual and metaphysical tradition emphasizes the importance of a continuing state of gratitude when it comes to staying connected with the universal source of all abundance. I find life is easier to accept when I look at my cup as half full, not half empty. Instead of focusing on what you don't have, focus on all the blessings you do have. Thank the universe for all the gifts bestowed upon you. It's okay to ask for more, but keep it simple and deal with one thing at a time. Don't get too greedy. Once you feel grateful for all the good you have in your life, you find contentment and peace. Our gratitude is like the rain that falls on the tree of abundance, nourishing it and allowing abundance to grow and flourish even more in our lives.

Above all, remember that abundance is all around us because it is the nature of the universe to be abundant. Just as we are surrounded by air, we are surrounded in the universe's unseen bounty. Taking it in is as natural as breathing, and we can and should use our inner wisdom to align ourselves with its riches.

So pay attention to signs, synchronicities, and coincidences. Listen to the people around you and check their advice with your own intuitive gut feelings. Find advisors who have the intuitive touch (a combination of experience and a willingness to listen to the part of them that knows without knowing how it knows). If you have a dream about lottery numbers or a horse that's going to win at the track, remember it's all about the interpretation of that dream. So go ahead and place a bet, but don't bet too much—and realize that you may need to bet the same numbers for a year before you win! Once you've used your logic and common sense, feel out the investment opportunities presented to you. If you hear the little voice saying, "Don't put your money into this," *obey it.* And above all, connect to abundance by being grateful for all that you have already received.

Finally, remember that money's good, but you can't take it with you. Money and power don't mean anything in the spiritual world. It's not how rich and famous we are, it's about the kind of life we lead. Thousands of years ago the philosopher Plato wrote "Grant that I may become beautiful in my soul within, and that all my external possessions may be in harmony with my inner self." Abundance is attracted to beauty, gratitude, and generosity of spirit, and these qualities will make your life more abundant whether you have one dollar or a hundred million dollars.

11

On the Side of the Angels

*You have the capacity to change the world within a moment.
All you must do is make a simple choice. Are you going to
choose a world of love and gratitude, or a tortured world filled
with discontent and impoverishment?*

—Masaru Emoto, *The Hidden Messages in Water*

Most of the messages I deliver from loved ones who have passed over are about love, peace, and healing, because that's what is most essential in the majority of relationships here on earth. The spirits I speak to offer consolation, encouragement, advice, apologies; they want to reach across the barrier and reassure those left behind that love never dies, and we will see the people we cared about again, when it's our turn to pass over. Like Corrie, a woman who was dying of breast cancer. Her mother and twin sister came through to tell her they would be waiting for her with open arms, and to tell Corrie's family that she would be all right after she passed. That brought so much reassurance and consolation to Corrie and her family. I was recently informed that Corrie passed on to the other side. I know she is happy with her mother and twin sister.

Then there was Marianne. Her son, Burt, had died while he was in his twenties, and she was devastated. I asked Marianne if she had had a dream about her son. "Yes—he said, 'I'm not dead, it was just a joke,' " she replied.

"It is a joke for people in the spirit world," I told her. "Because there is no death. Love is the bridge that connects us to the spirit world. His love still connects the two of you. And he wants you to enjoy life. Your son lived every day as if he was dying, so he lived it to the fullest. And it will make him happy if you do the same."

Those are the usual kinds of messages I receive from the other side. Our loved ones want us to treasure our time here and the love we share with each other. They come through me to tell the people here of their love and caring, because love is the greatest goodness we can know, and the only thing that will endure. Our dear ones continue to care for us, and we can continue to send them love with our thoughts, good wishes, and prayers. Spirits on the other side are only a thought away—when you bring them into your awareness, they know it. When the name or face of a loved one comes to mind, know that is her way of communicating with you, and send her your love in return.

Marianne's reading also demonstrates a different kind of message, but one that is equally important: we don't lose our personalities when we pass over. People don't automatically become all goodness, light, and forgiveness when they die, especially when they feel things were left undone or there was some injustice that occurred with their passing. I see this frequently with those who have met a violent death, or who have taken their own lives. Some of the saddest messages come from people who have committed suicide—not because they are "damned," but because these spirits now realize the mistake they made in ending their lives. Some souls are troubled and have a very hard time coping with life on this earth plane, but if they commit suicide before they finish their purpose for being here, they will have to keep coming back until they do. When people cut their lives short, they still have to grow, either in the spirit world or by being reincarnated. If they come back into other bodies, they still will have to learn the lessons their spirits missed from the lives they ended by suicide.

Each lifetime we live on this earth (and we can come back many, many times), we learn different sets of lessons that are all designed to help us grow. When we die, we review our life and see what we've done, right or wrong. Anything we've done wrong, we have to fix, and so we come back as someone else. For example, perhaps someone was a caveman and knocked his wife over the head with a club and killed her, leaving the children alone. In his next life, he could be a monk dedicated to his faith, who spends his days saving homeless children. The next life he could be a woman who has a happy life due to all the good this soul did as a monk. She has earned the right to be a mother, and maybe she raises a child who grows up to discover the cure for a devastating disease or who arranges an important peace treaty—something of true value to the world. Each time we complete a lifetime, we review our lives with the eyes of goodness and truth and then decide what lessons we will take on the next time.

We live many different lifetimes to learn the lessons that will help us elevate our soul to the highest level. But in each lifetime we have the choice—to grow or not to grow, to learn

the lessons or ignore them. Ultimately, yes, we are all supposed to be evolving to the point where we are completely
one with universal goodness, love, and wisdom. But that is the
destination; most of us, and most spirits, are still on the road
to perfection. Just because someone has passed over doesn't
mean he knows everything or even has your best interests at
heart. As there are good and bad people on earth, in the spirit
world there are good and bad people, and there are different
"neighborhoods" we can go to when we pass over. That is
why I say that spirits are like friends: they can give you good
advice or bad advice, and you have to choose what advice you
take. Don't fall into the trap of regarding someone else as the
final word. Don't take anyone's advice, including mine, without checking inside yourself to determine whether or not you
feel it is right. Author and psychologist Jean Houston once
said that the word *guru* really meant "gee, you are you." Your
inner wisdom is connected to divine, eternal energy just as
much as anyone else's. You must use its power to help you
chart your way upon this earth.

We create much of our destiny by the choices we make
in life. There is a plan, a map, for the experiences we will go
through when we come to earth, but we have choices as to
how we go through it. In the same way that there are many
different roads you can take to go from New York to California, there are different routes we can travel over the course of
our lives. In every moment we have free will as to which road
we take. Not all our destiny is etched in stone; instead, it is
formed in every moment by the lessons we're here to learn
and the choices we make.

Remember, your time here on earth will determine how
much progress you make on that road to perfection. What you

do in this life matters. How you treat people matters. The love you give to others, and the love they give to you, matters. It's okay to make mistakes as long as we learn from them; in fact, many times that's the only way we learn. When we die it's not important how famous or rich we are or how we look—it's our deeds that matter. Did we lead our lives well? Did we live with a clear conscience and with goodness and love and compassion for others? Could we look in the mirror every morning and live with ourselves? Our lives continue in the spirit world, and that's why it's so important for all of us to live our lives to the fullest, be the best we can be as people, because that is our only reason for being here.

Between Good and Evil

Our responsibility for being the best we can be extends far beyond ourselves, because every moment we are contributing to the good or the evil of the world. I've seen firsthand what the power of good can do, as well as the power of evil, because I've felt both in the readings I've done and in the spirits who have spoken with me from the other side. Several years ago I was sitting backstage, getting ready to record my very first TV show in Holland, when someone came in and told me that a politician named Pim had been assassinated. I didn't know who he was or anything about him, but I knew it was important. Because of the assassination, they postponed the airing of the TV show.

Several months later, I had the chance to read for Pim's brother, Martin. Right before we were scheduled to start the taping, all of a sudden a glass shattered onstage, and a shelf on the back wall of the studio fell down. I knew right away that that energy was Pim. I told Martin that while Pim's spirit was in a good place (he was with their grandmother, Marie, whose name and energy I picked up on), Pim was very angry and frustrated. "He wasn't able to finish his purpose on earth," I told Martin. "He only wanted to do good, but he was taken much too soon, before he could help people the way he wanted. Pim doesn't need me to get his message across. He will find whatever vehicle he needs to do it on his own."

"Don't worry about whoever committed this crime," I continued. "There is such a thing as karma. What comes around goes around. If you even think a negative thing, it can come back on you—maybe not from the same person, but it will come back. One day the universe will handle whoever did this. Your brother will get justice, if not in this world, then in the next."

Why do men and women choose the dark side? Why are there murders, terrorist attacks, adults abusing children? These are the eternal questions that I, as both a spiritual intuitive and a human being, have to wrestle with daily. My mother taught me long ago that one of the most important lessons is that even though it's hard, we must accept certain things in this world. I wish that lesson made it easier to understand the atrocities and suffering that occur. However, I do understand this: life is like a battery—it's made up of both positive and negative energy, and a battery doesn't run unless there's a positive and negative charge. For whatever reason there always has been good and evil, positive and negative energy, and it's up to us which energy we choose in any given moment. If our purpose on earth is to learn and grow, one of our greatest lessons is to use our power of choice wisely. Negative energy can be very tempting. Sometimes we're tested and tempted by "forbidden fruits." But goodness has more power than evil, even if most times you have to work harder for it to win.

Unfortunately, our past lives and the experiences we have in this one can sometimes cause us to tilt toward the negative energy. Children who were abused often grow up to abuse others. People who grow up in alcoholic families are more prone to substance abuse. If we didn't have loving and supportive parents, we can find it hard to form relationships. People also can choose negative energy because they're in the grip of trickster spirits. When we are physically or emotionally weakened, these spirits can influence us to do things we wouldn't otherwise do. Chemical dependency—drug abuse, alcohol, many kinds of addictions—can open us to these trickster energies, as well as causing us to take negative actions when we are under the influence of the addiction. We can shield ourselves from trickster energies by putting a white light of protection around ourselves and demanding that they go away. My friend Hetty, who is an intuitive and a healer, has people say out loud to the trickster energies, "You cannot have my power; I take back my power," and she tells them to really mean it when they say it.

One of the best ways to keep such energy away from us is to get help for any addictions or past traumas that may attract negativity. Therapy can help us see that we have choices. People who develop phobias or who are very hurt by the events of their lives often feel they have no other choice than to do evil. In those circumstances, evil may even seem like good to them. Good, effective psychotherapy can help people understand that there are other ways of thinking, being, responding. It can help people take another path and choose good.

The Greek philosopher Epictetus once wrote, "Seek not good from without: seek it within yourselves, or you will never find it." Good comes from within us, and it is put into form through our thoughts and deeds. Our thoughts create our reality. Thoughts are things. The thoughts we have as children will shape our thoughts as adults. Our thoughts as adults will shape our actions, and determine whether we choose goodness or evil, positive or negative energy.

Most of us know right from wrong; the number of sociopaths and psychokillers out there who don't know the difference is miniscule, compared to the billions of us who do. We're taught right from wrong as children, and I believe (and experience) that we also know right from wrong inside ourselves. We have to listen to the guidance we receive from inside ourselves and from the outside world. We all have a conscience, that little voice that whispers inside our hearts. I feel that conscience comes from a divine being—call it God, Buddha, the universe, Allah, Christ, Jehovah, Shiva, or any other name you wish. My parents told me love is God and God is love, and to this day that is what I believe. Our conscience represents that all-encompassing love and compassion and truth. It tells us to follow the one great commandment that is common to every religion and humanistic belief and to plain old common decency: "Do unto others as you would have them do unto you." For thousands of years the Golden Rule has been some of the best guidance we could have for how to choose the good and practice love and compassion.

We also need to stop judging others. The Bible says, "Judge not lest ye be judged." It seems to me that judgment leads to hatred, which always leads to evil. You can hate the sin, as most of us do. No one in his right mind could love the sin of child abuse, or terrorist attacks, or someone who murders another human being. But what good does it do to hate the person who commits the sin? Does it help that person choose not to do evil the next time? No. Does it make us any better as human beings? Not at all. Hate and self-righteousness are tearing the world apart right now. Hate is not a feeling that elevates our spirits. Masaru Emoto showed that the words *I hate you* can prevent water crystals from forming and cause rice to turn black and rot. We need to harness the power of our intuition, our minds, and our feelings and use them to make the world a better place rather than using them to hate others and bring the energy of the entire world down.

Mahatma Gandhi said, "Be the change you want to see in the world." That's our job. We must take the lead because we know and understand there's another way. This does not mean you must become a doormat and accept any negative energy someone is sending your way, or that you let people take advantage of you. If someone is treating you badly or trying to injure you somehow, don't hate him or take in his negative energy. Simply put up your white light of protection and let his energy bounce back toward him. And remember karma—he will live out the consequence of his deeds either in this life or the next.

Above all, we need to teach our children to cherish the power of their inner wisdom. Yes, we have to teach them how to protect themselves from negative energy, but we also need to help them hold onto the natural love, energy, and spirit they bring into the world. We must give them hope, support, and understanding. We need to educate them to live by the Golden Rule, to allow others to be free to believe as they wish, and above all, to connect to the inner wisdom that will be their first, best guide on the path they walk in this world. When we do that, our children will be more inclined to choose good over evil, light over darkness, and perhaps with them as our inspiration, we adults will choose goodness, too.

We Can Help Heal the World

I believe our progress along the path of positive life force is important not just for ourselves but also for the very future of our world. As human beings, we all have a joint responsibility to use our innate intuitive power to keep shifting the direction of the life force toward the light. We're at a time when the life force of the universe is changing, shifting, going into high gear. Certainly the energy of the planet is going through a metamorphosis, as can be seen with global warming, extreme weather, earthquakes of terrifying proportions, and climatic shifts that are causing devastation in one part of the world and record harvests in another. We see changes in energy manifesting as political conflict, terrorism, and local and national polarization. Social energy is shifting, too—I believe the turmoil and prejudice around social issues like gay marriage, abortion rights, even the debates about obscenity in our media are directly related to the turbulence of the universal life force.

There are many dark influences at work in the world. Poverty, fanaticism, greed, hatred, lying, disregard for the lives of others, contamination of our environment, are all pulling the earth's universal life force in a downward spiral that can only lead to destruction and despair. But it is equally true that every good thought, deed, feeling, intention, wish, and action takes us out of the darkness and lifts us higher. Each act of kindness is a rung on the ladder that you will climb on your journey to spiritual enlightenment. We can change our energy through our thoughts and deeds. And if enough of us elevate our energy, then maybe together we can change the energy of the planet.

In 1993 researchers conducted an experiment into the effects of group meditation on crime. Since 1979 groups of people who practice Transcendental Meditation have gathered daily to meditate on creating greater peace and harmony in the world. A study done in 1981 looked at the crime rates in forty-eight different cities. Twenty-four of these cities had reached the point where a full one percent of their populations practiced Transcendental Meditation on a regular basis. The other twenty-four cities didn't have that large a population of meditators. In the cities with the larger numbers of meditators, researchers noted the crime rate decreased by 22 percent. In the control cities (those with fewer meditators), crime increased by 2 percent. The cities with meditators experienced an 89 percent drop in the crime trend, versus an increase of 53 percent in the control cities.

Masaru Emoto, the wonderful man who wrote *The Hidden Messages in Water,* reminds us of our responsibility to raise the consciousness of the planet: "We have embarked on a new century, a time in history when we must make serious changes in the way that we think," he wrote. As residents on this remarkable planet at this remarkable time, we must be willing to open our minds and hearts and accept our responsibility as individual parts of this universal energy. We must be willing to help ourselves and help others move the direction of the life force toward the light and away from the darkness. We must be bold in our intentions and steadfast in our conviction that our actions, our thoughts, and our emotions *matter.* When we accept this power, all things are possible. And we, too, can change the world.

From the bottom of my heart I thank you for being open to your intuitive power and allowing me to share my insights with you. This has been my life's work for over thirty years—I feel that it's my purpose and my mission on the earth. It's a privilege to have a calling that brings peace to people and shows them their own greatness. May this book help you recognize and develop the inner wisdom that lies at your core and that links you with all the love, gratitude, and wisdom of the universe. May you learn to wield the power of this force to help raise us all toward the light.

References

Adrienne, Carol. *The Purpose of Your Life: Finding Your Place in the World Using Synchronicity, Intuition, and Uncommon Sense.* New York: Eagle Brook, 1998.

Ball, Aimee Lee. "Tantric Sex." *O, The Oprah Magazine,* March 2004.

Batie, Howard F. *Healing Body, Mind, & Spirit: A Guide to Energy-Based Healing.* St. Paul, Minn.: Llewellyn Publications, 2003.

Becker, Robert O., M.D., and Gary Selden. *The Body Electric: Electromagnetism and the Foundation of Life.* New York: William Morrow and Company, Inc., 1985.

Chopra, Deepak. *The Spontaneous Fulfillment of Desire: Harnessing the Infinite Power of Coincidence.* New York: Harmony Books, 2003.

Cohen, Andrew. "What is the Relationship Between Sex and Spirituality?" *What Is Enlightenment?* 13 (Spring–Summer 1998). (This issue focuses on sex and spirituality.)

Gladwell, Malcolm. *Blink: The Power of Thinking Without Thinking.* New York: Little, Brown and Company, 2005.

Goodwin, Marcus. *The Psychic Investor: Use Your Intuition Plus Investing Fundamentals to Profit in the Stock Market.* Holbrook, Mass.: Adams Media Corporation, 2000.

Groopman, Jerome, M.D. *Second Opinions: Stories of Intuition and Choice in the Changing World of Medicine.* New York: Viking Penguin, 2000.

Hiestand, Denie, and Shelley Hiestand. *Electrical Nutrition: A Revolutionary Approach to Eating That Awakens the Body's Natural Electrical Energy.* New York: Avery, 2001.

Klein, Gary. *The Power of Intuition: How to Use Your Gut Feelings to Make Better Decisions at Work*. New York: Doubleday, 2003. (Originally published under the title *Intuition at Work*.)

Koppel, Robert. *Intuitive Trader: Developing Your Inner Trading Wisdom*. New York: John Wiley & Sons, Inc., 1996.

Mike, Litman, and Jason Oman. *Conversations with Millionaires: What Millionaires Do to Get Rich, That You Never Learned About in School!* Reno, Nev.: Conversations with Millionaires, L.L.C., 2002.

Martin, Steve W. *Heavy Hitter Selling: How Successful Salespeople Use Language and Intuition to Persuade Customers to Buy*. Rancho Santa Margarita, Calif.: Sand Hill Publishing, 2004.

Emoto, Masaru. *The Hidden Messages in Water*. Translated by David A. Thayne. Hillsboro, Ore.: Beyond Words Publishing, Inc., 2004.

McTaggart, Lynne. *The Field: The Quest for the Secret Force of the Universe*. New York: HarperCollins, 2002.

Murphy, Joseph, Ph.D., D.D. *Think Yourself Rich: Use the Power of Your Subconscious Mind to Find True Wealth*. Paramus, N.J.: Reward Books, 2001. (Revised version of *Miracle Power for Infinite Riches*, published 1972.)

Myss, Caroline. *Sacred Contracts: Awakening Your Divine Potential*. New York: Three Rivers Press, 2002.

Myss, Caroline, Ph.D., and C. Norman Shealy, M.D. *The Creation of Health: The Emotional, Psychological, and Spiritual Responses That Promote Health and Healing*. New York: Three Rivers Press, 1988. Revised in 1993.

Nemeth, Maria, Ph.D. *The Energy of Money: A Spiritual Guide to Financial and Personal Fulfillment*. New York: Ballantine Publishing Group, 1997.

Orloff, Judith, M.D. *Positive Energy: 10 Extraordinary Prescriptions for Transforming Fatigue, Stress, and Fear into Vibrance, Strength, and Love*. New York: Harmony Books, 2004.

Patent, Arnold. *Money and Beyond*. Hillsboro, Ore.: Beyond Words Publishing, Inc., 1997.

Ramsdale, David, and Ellen Ramsdale. *Sexual Energy Ecstasy: A Practical Guide to Lovemaking Secrets of the East and West*. New York: Bantam Books, 1993.

Robinson, Lynn A. *Real Prosperity: Using the Power of Intuition to Create Financial and Spiritual Abundance*. Kansas City, Mo.: Andrews McMeel Publishing, 2004.

Schultz, Mona Lisa, M.D., Ph.D. *Awakening Intuition: Using Your Mind-Body Network for Insight and Healing*. New York: Three Rivers Press, 1998.

Targ, Russell, and Jane Katra, Ph.D. *Miracles of Mind: Exploring Nonlocal Consciousness and Spiritual Healing*. Novato, Calif.: New World Library, 1998.

Thibodeau, Lauren, Ph.D. *Natural-Born Intuition: How to Awaken and Develop Your Inner Wisdom*. Franklin Lakes, N.J.: The Career Press, Inc., 2005.

Tribole, Evelyn, M.S., R.D., and Elyse Resch, M.S., R.D., F.A.D.A. *Intuitive Eating: A Revolutionary Program that Works*. New York: St. Martin's Press, 1995. Revised in 2003.

Wilde, Stuart. *The Trick to Money Is Having Some*. Carson, Calif.: Hay House, 1989.

Acknowledgments

This book was long in the making and many people contributed to the effort. Thanks go to my amazing writer, Victoria St. George of Just Write, who knows how to put magic on paper even during the most challenging of times. Thanks also to my dedicated literary agent, Wendy Keller, of Keller Media Associates, who represents my books all over the world. In Los Angeles, I rely upon my trusted attorney, Chase Mellen III, and my television agent, Hayden Meyer, to guide me through complicated negotiations.

Thanks to Nancy Hancock and everyone at Simon & Schuster. I am delighted to be working with Carolyn Reidy and the super publicity team of Marcia Burch and Ellen Silberman. My warmest appreciation goes to Amanda Patten, my editor at Simon & Schuster. Thanks also to Maggie Hamilton at Allen Unwin in Australia for refining this book's title and for publishing my books in Oz. And a super huge thanks to my dear friend John Edward, who wrote the foreword.

I couldn't do what I do without my assistant, Steve Bilicki. Thanks, Steve, for your loyalty and tireless dedication. Also from my home base of Michigan, Judith Fussell and Marilyn Natchez provide valuable support. Enormous thanks also go to all the healers who keep my body and mind in top shape—Drs. Jeffrey Nusbaum and David Brownstein, Dr. Jeff Fantich, Dr. Robert Vinson, Hetty Quarella, Julie Abbou, Dr. Leonard Faye, Ann Hoffsteader, Dr. Denise Gordon, and Deana Geisler.

This book was first published in the Netherlands, following a run of very successful television shows. Many thanks to all my friends at RTL 4, including Kim Koppenol, Wim Ter Laak, Rik Luijcx, and Leo Van der Goot for making my TV shows so magical. I appreciate Lora Wiley, Borris Brandt, and John de Mol for getting me to Holland in the first place. Special thanks go to all my friends at Kosmos, including Maarten Carbo and Robbert Schuurmans for helping make *Discover Your Inner Wisdom* the number-one best seller in the Netherlands.

Many great media people in the United States have offered continuing support of my work, and I am extremely grateful. They include Wendy Walker, Larry King, and everyone at the *Larry King Live* show; Joanne Salzman, Regis Philbin, and everyone at *Live with Regis and Kelly;* Brad Bessey, Linda Bell Blue, Bonnie Tiegel, and Cheryl Woodcock at *Entertainment Tonight* and *The Insider;* Terry Wood, Carla Pennington, and Robin McGraw at Paramount; Dorothy Lucey and everyone at *Good Day L.A.;* Jackie Olensky, Katie Murphy, Sarah Goldsmith, everyone at Freemantle U.S., and my darlings Stuart Krasnow, Freddy Risher, and Derby Krasnow.

My family is the rock upon which I stand. Thanks and love to my sisters, Alicia Tisdale and Elaine Lippitt, and their families—Paul Tisdale, David Lippitt, Larry, Carolyn, Ronna, Linda, Lenny, Robin, Jason, Rachel, Lauren, Jordon, and Ryan—and to Katherine Jeffereys, who helped raise me. Thanks also to my friends including Bob Sher, Jon Hirsh, Malcolm Mills, Becky Geyer and her family, Mary and Harold Sarko, Linda Solomon, Danny Fantich, Mindy Levine, Gail Yancocek, Tisi Aylward, Alana Emhardt, Garth Ancier, Pennie Clark, Irena Medavoy, Lauren King, Chantal Cloutier, Craig Tomashoff, Diana Basehart and the rest (you know who you are!). And special thanks go to Brian and Carol Weiss, who have supported me in my career as a psychic intuitive.

This book would not exist without my clients, like Mike and Chris Blackman and many more, who give me the privilege of reading for them. They open their hearts and allow me to do the same. Thanks to all who shared their stories with me and gave me the privilege of being their bridge from this world to the next. Finally, thanks to my students who have come to me to help them learn to use their own inner wisdom. As I was teaching you, I have learned so much at the same time. I hope we will continue to learn together for many years to come.